DOGUE
contents

KU-009-998

BEAUTY AND HEALTH

Shapely news

Head start!

Elements of charm

TRAVEL

DOGS ARE BARKING ABOUT

IN EVERY ISSUE

reader letters

Arf Aid for Chinese dogs
I have just finished reading your fine article about the plight of dogs in Peking. It is a sorry state of affairs when a government turns against an innocent faction of its own country. I hadn't realized that half the city's dog population, 200,000 strong, had been heartlessly slaughtered or exiled to areas outside the city. This was done in anticipation of the ruling that dogs found living with people within the city of Peking would incur a fine equal to three weeks' wages. The only canines permitted to remain in the city were circus performers, police dogs, dogs living with foreign residents, and dogs participating in scientific experiments.

I feel that we should extend our help to our foreign brothers and sisters. Many are homeless and starving. I propose that a media event be created to draw attention to this tremendous problem and to raise funds to help these unfortunate animals. Perhaps a great dog show could be staged, with all entry fees and prizes donated to these truly needy dogs. It could be televised internationally to create greater awareness of the situation. If other readers feel as I do, please contact me, care of this magazine, so that we can make this dream a reality.
Bark Geldog
Los Angeles, CA

Hollywood and Oscar: anti-dog prejudice?
I want to commend you on your excellent review of the film *Down and Out in Beverly Hills*. You were correct in your assessment of Mike, the dog star of the picture, as perhaps the most promising new performer in Hollywood today. You were not alone in that opinion. Many reviewers from a variety of media felt exactly the same way. It is for this reason that I question the omission of Mike's name at Oscar nomination time. Why was he overlooked? Could this be a sign of anti-dog prejudice rearing its ugly head? Let's hope that Mike was not passed over for this reason, or, equally distressing, because the members of the Academy were jealous of his success (which has also been hinted about you-know-which-famous-director). It is too late to correct this situation for this year's award, but let's strive to see that next year's nominees are chosen fairly, according to merit, without regard to race, color, or breed.
Terri Grrr
Hollywood, CA

Tropical delights: con and pro
I am usually quite pleased with the tasteful photography which graces your pages, but last issue was a nightmare for me and my young puppies. I am referring to the article on tropical vacations. You had the poor taste to include a photograph of dogs sunning at a nude beach. To find unclad animals of both sexes lounging together in suggestive poses in the pages of *Dogue* is shocking. My puppies saw the photos and began to ask all sorts of unanswerable questions. I am left no choice but to cancel my subscription to your magazine, effective immediately.
Phyllis Shih-Tzu
Peoria, IL

I was so happy to see you exercise some artistic license in your last issue. Usually your travel coverage is fairly staid—descriptions of the new exhibit at the local dog museum, and all that. I was glad, therefore, to see you behave in a more contemporary manner in your latest choice of vacation spot—the tropical islands. Your descriptions were so inviting, I can hardly wait to hop on a plane! The photos were equally attractive—all those beautiful animals glowing in the sunlight! I know where I'm headed this winter, thanks to you.
Princess Maier
New York

Lucky: the ups and downs of public life
Well, it seems that the lives of the rich and famous are not so different, after all. I'm referring to your article about Lucky, the First Dog. Or shall I now say, Second Fiddle? Since your coverage of Lucky's happy antics at the White House, I was shocked to hear about his apparent fall from grace. He's been banished to the Reagans' Santa Barbara ranch in deference to the new First Dog, Rex, a canine more suitable in size and demeanor to petite Nancy R. While I'm sure that Lucky is being well looked after in California, it's a bit sad to see him whisked away from the public eye. But, as in all things, I guess that's how it goes—heir today, gone tomorrow.
Spike Tyler
Uhlerstown, PA

Slender Vittles for vim and vigor
I am a working dog with little free time on my paws. I have a high-profile position with a Fortune-500 company and do a lot of entertaining for business—dinners out, and such. A quiet dinner at home is a rare treat, and I look forward to the evenings spent alone in my own doghouse. The business dinner circuit has taken its toll on my figure, and I've put on a few pounds too many. Work leaves me dog tired and not enough time to shop for and prepare a healthy low-calorie dinner. Therefore, I tend to chow down a box of biscuits in front of the T.V. or munch on a bowlful of treats. These are tasty and easy to eat, but junk food doesn't satisfy my body's need for a balanced diet. You can imagine, then, my pleasure in reading about the new convenience foods mentioned in your last issue. At last, microwave meals for yuppie puppies! Low-calorie Slender Vittles have made a real difference in my life . . . and to my figure. The easy-to-heat, easy-to-eat pouches of food can be zapped warm in seconds. What will they think of next? I bet it won't be long before we see low-calorie meals like these in supermarkets for *people*!
Annabel Oschmann
Houston, TX

No bad dogs—just bad people
Barbara Doghouse is correct when she writes that there are "no bad dogs, only inexperienced owners." Indeed, I believe that most of us take great pride in our good behavior and loyalty to our human companions. Many misdirected people confuse us with their inconsistent directions, and then they react badly when they perceive us to be unruly or unresponsive. If only people would read Mrs. Doghouse's book! Only then would we be assured of a fair shake in life and no longer be blamed for mistakes that occur through no fault of our own. People, wise up! Listen to your dogs, for you can learn something from them.
Mortimer Grievson
London, England

I was surprised to read your recent review of Barbara Doghouse's *No Bad People*. This inflammatory treatise is rife with the highest form of prejudice and anti-dog sentiment that I have ever seen. The book promotes the theory that all people are basically good and fair, and that it is our carelessness and mischievous behavior which are responsible for people's disciplinary actions toward their dogs.

I have never known a dog to deliberately mistreat people. Most of Mrs. Doghouse's cases of misbehavior were simply a wrong interpretation of dogs' good intentions. Take the example of the dog who chewed a pair of his person's slippers. The dog felt that his owner deserved a *new* pair of slippers, and this was the only way he could convey the message. The story of the dog who refused to walk outside on cold or wet days . . . he was simply saving his person from the unnecessary nuisance of going outside in inclement weather. The dog who dug a hole in the wall of the living room was merely defending his family from the onslaught of insect invaders. So you see, these dogs were behaving in a kind and helpful manner. The negative slant of the book would suggest quite the contrary. *Dogue* does not usually promote the work of people, and particularly those who seek to malign the good reputation of dogs. I was surprised to see this sudden change in viewpoint, and hope it does not reflect a new policy at *Dogue*. In the future I hope you will continue to support issues and attitudes which convey dogs in a positive light.
Simone de Bouvier
Paris, France

fITNESS NOW

Are you a round hound? Or are you simply a pudgy puppy with some baby fat to burn?

Here's news. The Jane Fidos of the doggy set, Warren and Faye Eckstein, have written a new diet and exercise book, *Pet Aerobics* (Henry Holt and Company, $14.95), and the exercise program contained therein includes workout routines to benefit any animal in any physical shape.

Dogue takes delight in featuring two simple exercises from the book—the Sit-Up and the Push-Up. (As with all forms of exercise, it is important to see your veterinarian for a stress test before beginning any new workout program.)

• **The Sit-Up:** The dog sit-up is a repetition of two simple commands—"sit" and "up." By obeying these commands in sequence, you can enjoy a health-benefiting workout while your owner goes through the rigors of human sit-ups. As we all know, exercise is more fun when you have a gym buddy.

(1) At the command of "sit," you sit in place, folding your hind legs at the knees and setting your bottom on the floor.

(2) At the command of "up," you stand up on all fours, at attention.

Practice "sit" and "up" until you feel comfortable with the commands and are able to perform them in sequence, as shown in the photographs. Build up a brisk rhythm.

Bruce Morgan

• **The Push-Up:** The dog push-up is also a repetition of two simple commands: "sit" and "down." You have already perfected the "sit" command (1) described in the last exercise. But now you have to learn to follow the command, "down."

(3) From the "sit" position, slide your front paws forward until your body is flat on the floor **(4)**. Now all you have to do is to return to the sitting position—which you do at the command of "up." Once again, work towards doing a series of these movements in repetition, preferably accompanied by your person who can more than likely benefit from several sets of human push-ups.

These routines, combined with a healthy low-calorie diet and other exercises chosen from the Ecksteins' *Pet Aerobics*, will turn even the plumpest pup into a fetching Fido!

groomers—a cut above the rest...

The best beauty looks begin with the right haircut. Some lucky dogs have hair that always seems to fall into place without the help of a brush or scissors. The rest of us must rely upon the right treatment from a qualified dog groomer. Select your groomer with care, and the time spent being washed and clipped will be well worth your investment.

the sweet smell of success...

Exude an air of confidence when you wear the latest perfume for pups—Four Paws Cologne. The distinctive black bottle makes an elegant addition to your boudoir, and the fragrance makes a lovely addition to your aura that will really keep the men on your tail. Breathe easily, knowing you smell good. Ah, the smell of it. . . .

what's new, bright eyes?

White-coated dogs are particularly susceptible to unsightly red or brown tear stains under their eyes. But white *can* be bright! Several brands of tear stain remover are currently on the market. Two brands to look for are Diamond Eye and Eye Brite. These and other remedies are available from your groomer or local pet supply store.

COVER LOOK

Play-Dead Glamour . . . the way to look for evening. A look that relies on more than simply being bright-eyed and bushy-tailed . . . The difference begins with attitude . . . hard work that looks easy . . . A good haircut is critical . . . combined with impeccable grooming to keep even the whitest hair looking luminous. The specifics, Town & Country Dogs Medicated Shampoo, a rich lathering, non-irritating formula which brightens coats without leaving a medicinal odor. Town & Country Dogs, London, England. Cocktail hat, Karl Dogerfeld for Dogwear, New York. Necklace, Bulldogari for Dogwear, New York. Hair, Richard Hiller. Photograph by Peter Serra, New York.

BEAUTY Q&A

Hair cure for K-9s. . . pedicure procedures . . . the white way to look bright. . .

Q I am a Yorkshire Terrier with dry fly-away hair. My hair always seems to be falling into my eyes, making it difficult for me to see, and giving me a rumpled and careless appearance. How can I achieve a fresher more pulled-together look?

A Yorkshire Terriers are not alone in having this problem, although it may be more pronounced in a delicately framed, petite dog like yourself. The solution can be found in several ways. Visit a qualified dog groomer who can suggest a hair style more in keeping with your hair length and texture.

One idea is a perky topknot or ponytail which captures the hair from the outside corners of your eyes to your ears, and all the hair over your eyes on your forehead. This is a classic style for Yorkies and can be made even more fashionable by the addition of a pretty flower or bow over the elastic band.

Be sure to use a covered elastic band or a tiny rubber one (similar to those provided with human tooth-braces), as the multiple wrapping of a rubber band around the ponytail can exert too much tension on delicate hair, resulting in broken and fly-away strands.

Another solution involves a change in hairstyle, with bangs being clipped over your eyes. This is an informal look and should not be considered by dogs in the show circuit as it is not an accepted style for judging.

Q My toenails are growing far too long. I am frightened to have them trimmed because I have seen friends bleed when their nails were cut too short. What should I do?

A Toenail trimming should not be an ordeal if done correctly. The key is to use the right equipment, a nail trimmer designed especially for a dog's toenails. It also helps to understand the anatomy of canine toes and nails.

The dog's toenails contain blood vessels and the delicate tips of their toes. The excess nail forms a slightly curved point below this portion of the toe. Following the directions provided with the toenail clipper, hold the foot firmly in place, and be careful not to cut too much from the tip of the nail. Special styptic pencils are available to stop any bleeding which may occur, but this should not happen if the job is done correctly.

The faint of heart may prefer to delegate this job to the dog groomer or veterinarian.

Q I am a West Highland White Terrier who is presently not so white. I have tried shampooing, but my coat still looks discolored and stained. What can I do to restore my coat to its former beauty?

A You did not say if your coat was discolored all over or if you suffer from individual stains. The first thing to do is to wash with a shampoo specially formulated for white coats. Some of these products contain a safe but mild bleaching agent or blue rinse to combat the yellowing of white hair.

If individual stains still remain, one cure involves applying a mild mixture of lemon juice and salt to the stain and rinsing off. This combination has been particularly effective in the removal of food stains from mouths and beards.

One final idea is the application of a professional groomer's white chalk to give the illusion of extra whiteness to the coat. The chalk comes in solid and powder formulations. It can even be mixed with a small quantity of water to form a paste which can be painted on to conceal stubborn spots.

If your coat does not respond to these simple home cures, it would be best for you to consult a groomer for more professional help.

Q My hair is medium length and very dry and fly-away. It never seems to stay in place. What can I do?

A You can treat this problem nutritionally with the addition of more fats to your diet, or with one of the many dietary supplement products which are commercially available to combat this problem.

The inconvenience of fly-away hair can also be treated externally. Are you bathing too frequently? This may result in dry skin and hair. Be sure to use a cream rinse or hair conditioner after your final rinse to reapply the necessary oils you may have removed during shampooing.

Spray-on grooming treatments also give hair a shiny gloss and make it more manageable. Their pleasant fragrance may also make it possible for you to extend the period of time between shampoos, resulting in less drying of your hair.

Pet therapy: learn to heal . . . teaching your people to obey simple commands . . . the cure for fleas: dippity dog. . . .

PET FACILITATED THERAPY— Mental Health for Dogs and Their Human Friends

A growing number of doctors, psychologists, and social workers agree that lonely and introverted people—the elderly, the mentally-disturbed, and convicts—can benefit from the companionship of an animal. Studies indicate that in addition to human/animal interaction, stroking and petting an animal can lower a person's blood pressure to below its resting level and can provide a general improvement in morale. All dogs should be alert to the fact that this is one medical benefit we can provide to our human companions.

Bashkim Dibra of Fieldston Dogs in Riverdale, New York, has begun a pioneering Pet Facilitated Therapy Program in conjunction with several nursing homes. Mr. Dibra, who is a professional trainer of celebrity animals, including the pets of Al Pacino, Carly Simon, and Robert Redford, also works with the Animal Medical Center in Manhattan to adapt pet programs for the retarded. This expert on human/animal interaction, can be called upon to consult about forming a personalized program for yourself or for a local institution. A member of the Council on Pets in Health-Related Facilities, he can be reached at (212) 796-4541 if you require further information about pet therapy programs.

PET PALS—Purina program pairs dogs with older adults

Dogs, do you want to adopt a human, age 60 or older? If so, you will be doing him or her a world of good because studies show that the companionship of a pet can bring down human blood pressure, reduce stress, and speed up recovery from an illness. The Pets for People program matches animals, one year or older, from local humane societies, with senior citizens. Dogs selected for the program arrive with their own collar and leash, food and water bowls, and a coupon for a three-month supply of dog food. In addition, the program pays the expenses for spaying or neutering, the initial veterinary visits, and innoculations. If you know of a human who would like to participate in this unique program, have him write to Purina Pets for People, Checkerboard Square, St. Louis, Missouri 63105.

celebrity dog trainers and trainers of celebrity dogs

People think that when we misbehave we need the services of a qualified dog trainer. Their assumption is only *half* right. *They* need the training to better understand how to communicate with *us*.

If training problems crop up between you and your people, a trainer should be consulted before the problem begins to get out of hand. Your veterinarian can suggest a reputable trainer, but you might wish to secure the services of the trainers and animal behaviorists to the stars. Among the best are

- Bashkim Dibra (212) 796-4541
- Warren Eckstein (516) 764-2683
- Brian Kilcommons (212) 722-0412
- Peter Borchelt (718) 275-9505

Warren Eckstein is also the author of a new book on pet therapy and behavior training called *Understanding Your Pet* (Henry Holt and Company, $16.95) and has produced a line of animal training kits, including kits for dog chewing and dog housebreaking. For more information about these kits, contact him at P.O. Box 422, Oceanside, New York 11572, or call (516) 764-2683.

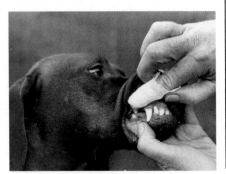

Open Wide and Say "Arf": The way to canine dental health

Don't let bad breath spoil your social life. Dog-O-Dontics are specially treated tooth cleaning pads that remove the plaque that causes bad breath and gum disease. They are easy to use. All you need is a person and one of his fingers! The pads wrap around a human finger, which then wipes over your teeth. It's easy! Dog-O-Dontics were developed by Joanne B. Wilson, a registered dental hygienist and the president of Canine Dental Health. They are veterinarian-approved and can be ordered from Canine Dental Health, P.O. Box 3955, Santa Barbara, California 93130. For information, call (805) 682-5717.

The Space-Age Cure for an Age-Old Problem: The electronic flea collar

The Micotech flea collar repels fleas within a four-foot radius safely. It uses P.M.B.C. (pulsed, modulated, burst circuit) sound, a high-frequency pitch which is 1000 cycles above the hearing level of a dog, and well out of range of human ears. Veterinarian-endorsed and 100 percent safe for dogs and humans, the Microtech collar will drive fleas away within five days and keep them off. It is available in two sizes, 18″ and 24″, with an adjustable web collar. The Microtech collar is carried by The Sharper Image stores and by mail through the same company's catalog. It lists for $59 and can be ordered by dialing, toll free, (800) 344-4444 and charging to a major credit card.

The Ancient Cure for the Same Age-Old Problem: Herbal flea collar and flea dip to prepare at home

Noah's Kingdom is the producer of a fine line of all-natural pet products, including foods, shampoos, vitamins, and more. The firm has been kind enough to provide us with these recipes for herbal flea dip and a flea collar to make at home. Noah's Kingdom is located at 622 Broadway, Suite 4A, New York, New York 10021, (800) 223-7503, or, in New York, (212) 473-3800.

FLEA DIP

Mix the following essential oils in equal proportions, and use *sparingly* (8 to 10 drops in one gallon of water). Use after shampooing and let the animal drip dry. These oils work as repellants because of their aromatic properties. *They are very strong:*

Penny Royal	Cedar Wood
Eucalyptus	Citronella

FLEA COLLAR

Buy a fabric or leather collar and a small paint brush. Spread on enough of *each* of the following oils to cover the collar, and then let dry:

1 oz. Citronella Oil	1 oz. Eucalpytus Oil
1 oz. Penny Royal Oil	1 oz. Calendula Oil

THE GREAT DOGHOUSE IN THE SKY: helping humans cope with loss

It is hard enough to consider our eventual exit from this vale of tears, but what about our poor human companions who will be left behind? How will they deal with the loss of our friendship and presence?

To get them over this painful period, two great veterinary institutions have begun pioneering pet bereavement programs. Susan Cohen is a social worker at New York's Animal Medical Center. She came there in 1982 to help people adjust to a pet's illness or death. Jamie Quackenbush is the pet bereavement counselor at the University of Pennsylvania's Center for the Interaction of

Animals and Society. These social workers conduct programs and offer individual counseling to people who are having trouble coping with the loss of a pet. If these facilities are not convenient to where you live, your local veterinarian may be able to help. Ask him about the brochure "Pet Loss and Human Emotion," published by the Animal Veterinary Medical Association. Better still, secure a copy and keep it with your toys and other precious possessions. It will be there for human eyes once that inevitable day arrives. . . .

COMPUTER DATING — Kal Kan Selectadog Program matches people with their dream dog

The Kal Kan Company has devised a brief questionnaire to help people choose the right breed of dog to conform to their particular lifestyle. The Selectadog questionnaire asks seventeen short but pertinent questions, including "How active are you? (infirm, not very, quite, or very)," "Do you need a protector dog or just a warning bark?" and "What size should your dog be? (toy, small, medium, large." The form must be returned to Kal Kan, and a list of appropriate dog breeds will be suggested. To send for a copy of this survey, write to Kal Kan Selectadog, 3386 East 44th Street, Vernon, California 90058-0853.

WALK IN SAFETY AND COMFORT

Flexi leashes offer a dog flexibility for daily walks. The self-retracting leash has an instant brake control and means no more pulling, sags, or tangles. The three basic models (1: for toy dogs up to 10 pounds, 2: for medium dogs up to 30 pounds, and 3: for dogs over 31 pounds) extend to 16 feet and are available in a selection of several colors. Flexi leashes were designed in Germany over ten years ago, but are now available throughout the United States and Great Britain. They can be purchased at local pet stores, or contact the Flexi Company for the location of a store nearest you: Flexi America, 437 Rockaway Avenue, Valley Stream, New York 11581, (516) 825-11581; Flexi England, c/o Mr. Ronald Gee, 2 Hove Place, Hove, Sussex BN3 2RG, (0273) 728331/2.

have a heart: EKGs for dogs

A New York veterinary cardiologist has developed a simplified method for determining a dog's heart rate without the use of or investment in expensive diagnostic equipment. Dr. Robert Cohen has initiated the Cardiopet system for veterinarians without electrocardiogram machines. He has made it possible to give EKG tests to animals over the telephone! Hundreds of veterinarians now subscribe to the service, which operates in this manner: Wires are painlessly clipped to the patient's legs. The wires are attached to a transmitter which relays the heartbeat via telephone to Cardiopet in New York. A written report will arrive from Cardiopet within two days, or in emergency situations the results can be obtained within an hour.

Rufflon introduces Super Lustrous Creme Nail Enamel. Toenails will never be the same . . .

What's the ugliest part of your body? Some say your toes . . . We say, no more!

Toes become totally terrific when colored with Rufflon's new toenail enamel. The range of colors will leave you breathless and panting for more . . . New tones will be introduced to complement each season's latest fashions.

Rufflon nail enamel paints on smooth and dries quickly . . . No more smears when digging up your bones . . .

Rufflon. The difference between dog and hot dog, bow and wow.

h AIR NOW

Shampoos and conditioners to suit every coat

Hair to the throne . . . treatments with an English accent . . . what's hot . . . French bred . . . shampoo highlights . . . a coat of many colors

THE CRUFTS COAT

London's Town & Country Dogs is the producer of a fabulous new line of hair-care products, formulated by Marian Edsor, former chief chemist to the internationally famous beauty house of Helena Rubinstein. The products, fully tested in the strictly confined circumstances of the British Quarantine Stations, are the hair-care products selected by the top winners of the world-renowned Crufts Championship Dog Show.

The line includes two shampoo formulas—Medicated Shampoo and Enriched Shampoo with Wheatgerm Oil—and five different conditioning sprays—True De-Tangle Spray, Grooming Spray, Super Sheen Spray (for short-haired dogs), Real High Gloss Spray (for wire-haired dogs), and Hold & Style Spray. Each is available from Town & Country Dogs, 35B Sloane Street, London S.W.1, (01) 730-5792. In the United States, write Town & Country Dogs, P.O. Drawer 608, Monroeville, Alabama 36461, or call (205) 743-2828.

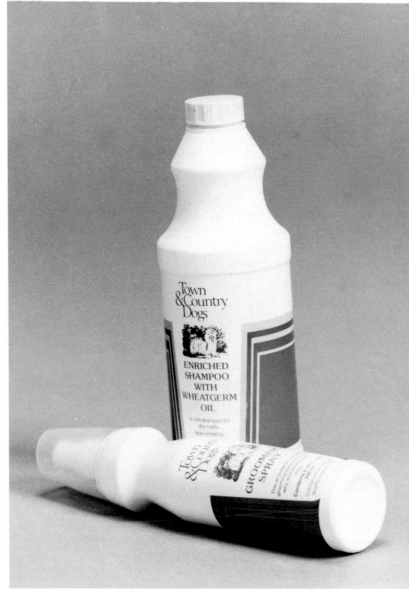

THE POODLE CUT: A FRENCH TWIST

Parisian puppies are known for a certain *je ne sais quoi*. They can usually sniff a trend before it hits our shores. *Dogue's* Parisian editors have discovered a small, local beauty salon which caters to the most fashionable Fifi's around. *Le Petit Monde du Chien*, at 14 rue des Bernadins in trendy St. Germain, has been turning out some of the most current cuts in Paris. The shop also carries a small line of its own hair-care products to keep its customers Poodle Perfect. Dogs of all breeds come here when they want to look their best. Parisians say "oui, oui" to Le Petit Monde du Chien. You'll say "ooh-la-la."

CHERRYBROOK—THE PICK OF THE PRODUCTS

Looking for a hard-to-find grooming aid or pet supply? Uncertain which shampoo formula would be best for you? Cherrybrook is the largest canine wholesale supply company in the United States. The firm carries over 1,600 items from 151 manufacturers, and the list keeps growing. A simple call to Cherrybrook's toll-free number, (800) 524-0820, puts you in touch with people who are knowledgeable about dogs and their welfare. Cherrybrook is the supplier of choice to the American dog show circuit, and it is easy to see why. The firm's current catalog lists no fewer than 130 different shampoos and rinses, 67 coat sprays and dressings, and 21 chalks and powders to enhance color. Cherrybrook is located at Route 57, Box 15, Broadway, New Jersey 08808; the phone number in New Jersey is (201) 689-7979.

SHAMPOOS: A RAINBOW OF CHOICES

The major hair-care manufacturers recognize that all dog hair is not alike. Hair of different color, length, and texture responds best to shampoos and conditioners specially formulated for their unique differences. Shampoos and conditioners are also designed to soothe irritated skin, kill fleas and parasites, smell fresh, not burn eyes, and to be used without water. The choices easily rival the selections available for people!

Many makers manufacture a full range of products keyed to hair color. White hair can be brightened, apricot and brown coats can be enhanced, and silver and black coats can sparkle with the application of the correct shampoo formula. Manufacturers producing a line of color-enhancing shampoos for some or all of these hair colors include Lambert Kay, Four Paws, Ring 5, Hagen, Oster, Mr. Groom, House of An-Ju, Tomlyn, and Pro Line. These products, and others, are available at your local pet supply store.

Beauty & the beast

FROM REAL DOG TO DIVINE IN A BEAUTY MAKEOVER

Are you tired of looking like a dirty dog? Is it time for a new image?

April, the toy Poodle pictured here, has beautiful classic features which are hidden by her drab and shapeless hairdo. We asked hair expert Jenny McDonagh, of Karen's for People and Pets in New York, to create a special cut for April . . . to maximize her beauty potential.

April's coat is rinsed in preparation for shampooing.

The shampoo is applied. A special no-tears formula is used to protect delicate eyes.

The shampoo is rinsed off and followed with a conditioner for manageability and shine.

The result—a dramatic difference. April is transformed into a real Yankee Poodle Dandy! Special touches include colorful ribbon bows tied on to accent the beautiful contours of the cut.

Karen's for People and Pets is located at 1220 Lexington Avenue, New York, New York 10028, (212) 472-9440.

April's hair is fluffed by hand under a dryer.

The coat is brushed smooth prior to the haircut.

April's hair is precision cut to give volume and style.

Hank Londoner

color me bow wow:

New options in nail polish and hair color . . . American Gruffiti: a palette of possibilities to bring out the real you . . . Pop and Punk effects to color by number . . . theatrical makeup to set you at center stage.

An explosion of color is the newest trend to hit the beauty business. The quickest way to pop up a look is with an infusion of color. A full range of temporary hair-color products is now available. The instant colors come in a variety of forms—sprays, mousses, and gels—but all can be used effectively to create a rainbow of new fashion looks.

Color gels or mousses can be stroked on in dots or stripes; the holding action of these products can be used effectively to hold up small tufts, spikes, or ridges of fur. The spray-on colors can be applied free-form style for a look reminiscent of American Gruffiti! The more creative of us may choose to cut out stencils of simple shapes (dots, stars, and small Scottie dogs are favorites) and spray on color over these for a more precise line.

Unfortunately, these color products are new on the market and are not yet available at pet supply stores. They *can* be found where people buy their hair treatments and in most beauty supply stores. Exercise caution when applying these products, taking care not to use them on the face or near the eyes. The colors shampoo out, so they can be used to create a special look for an evening and be easily removed the next day.

Nail color is another way to add color to contemporary fashion. Gerard/Pellham has created a nail-color line called Ultracoat that is especially for pets. The polish dries in thirty seconds to prevent smearing, and comes in fifteen colors, including Fifth Avenue Pink, Key West Lemon, and Worth Avenue Blue. The polish is available at your local pet supply store.

Special effects to try include matching or contrasting your nail color to the color of your outfit, hair ribbons, or collar. Try painting each nail a different color for a rainbow effect.

If pet nail polish cannot be found in your area, you can achieve the same spectacular results with any brand of people nail color.

Be bold! Be colorful! Paint yourself pretty today!

Canine Klein

PLAY DEAD GLAMOUR: THE NEW FASHION DOGMA

Elegance is the key to the new extravagance. Dogs are dressing up again, and it's a welcome change from the informality of the past. No longer content with the rudimentary basics of apparel —Checkers' respectable Republican cloth coat, as it were—today's fashion hound looks to the top dogs of government, business, the arts, and entertainment to give the fashion command.

HAIL TO THE CHIEFS

Some say the White House has helped set the tone. The emergence of Rex, the First Dog, as a public figure has put well-groomed dogs in the spotlight. He marks a departure from the low-keyed house dogs of administrations past. Other dogs in the Reagan power structure have also achieved a degree of social prominence. C. Fred Bush, Vice President George Bush's dog, is a best-selling author, having published *C. Fred's Story* a few years back. Another group of canine celebrities sponsor the Capitol Canine Follies and Fair as a fund-raising event for the Capitol Children's Museum. These movers and shakers are at present in the vanguard of the new era of dog fashion. For Rex and the remainder of the well-dressed pack, *haute couture* is all. Harvey, Prince Charles' and Princess Diana's Labrador Retriever, also has quite a wardrobe. Whenever Princess Di orders a new dress, she asks the designer to make a matching scarf for Harvey. And, of course, the Queen's Corgis walk the corridors of power at the kennels of Balmoral and Sandringham.

JUMPING UP THE SOCIAL LADDER

The new social mobility has given dogs a reason to dress up again. A full range of social activities relating to the upscale lifestyle has created the need for a more fully developed fashion wardrobe. Designers have risen to the occasion to provide us with more dressing options than ever before.

YUPPIE PUPPIES DRESS FOR SUCCESS

"Well-dressed" means more than a quick flick of the brush and donning a rhinestone collar. The upwardly mobile dog has choices to make. At our paws are a full spectrum of designers who are creating looks suitable for every lifestyle and level of taste. From leisure wear to formal attire, every occasion is being met with a selection of designs to please any dog's needs.

WORKING LIKE A DOG

Dogs have joined the ranks of the working world. More dogs are employed in business than ever before, and the range of professions is endless. Whether they be involved in civil service, police work, the military, the arts, film, or fashion, **the business animal has special needs which must be met.** Clothes have to be beautiful and suitable for the work place. Comfort and easy care are two other important features in clothing for the working animal.

GRABBING LIFE BY THE TAIL

Working dogs and others have come to value their free time as more precious than before. The quality of life achieved here often has to surpass the quantity of time. Dogs are using their free time to travel, participate in the arts, exercise, go out, or simply to sit at home and watch a good movie or program on TV. Contemporary designers are addressing this range of needs with creativity and a sense of humor.

GOOD TASTE EXTENDS BEYOND THE DOG DISH

Fashions are making a bold statement this season. No longer content to live on the fringe, dogs are expressing their good taste in the choice of elegant garments constructed of beautiful fabrics. Attention is given to quality and detail. Precision of fit is important, and versatility is key. Garments can be dressed up or down with the addition of accessories, and every dog is beginning to amass a collection of special collars and neckpieces.

HUMAN COPYCATS ARE GOING TO THE DOGS FOR INSPIRATION

Canine couture is seen as the cutting edge of fashion. Indeed, even human designers are beginning to adapt the key looks and silhouettes into scaled-up versions for people! That's not surprising, because, as we've always known, in the walk of life, man invariably follows dog. . . .

19

THE NEW YORK COLLECTIONS

The time has come for a change in fashion. A new simplicity of design. Clothes that are the essence of line. Pared down to the basic elements. The new freedom in dressing, the new ease, is a reflection of the American sportswear tradition. Classic combinations of clear colors, crisp fabrics . . . done best by the New York designers who embody the All-American look.

Canine Klein is celebrated for his clean lines . . . sculptural forms which skim over the body, revelling in its perfection. This relaxed yet upbeat outfit, *right*, follows all the new rules. Cool linen is sashed by leather at the hip. The slim skirt is an unexpected counterpoint to the fullness of the top. The colors evoke sunlight— cream, peach, gold—and enliven any complexion. To order, Dogwear, 611 Broadway, Suite 702, New York City 10012, (212) 533-0717; Town & Country Dogs, 35b Sloane Street, London S.W.1, (01) 235-6714.

Sportswear of the moment, with the kind of timeless appeal that goes on and on . . . Case in point, *opposite page*: Puppy Ellis brings us a new twist on the tuxedo. Forget the lapels—satin gleams *everywhere*. Bloused in fuchsia, sashed in red. The black skirt is the only bow to convention. Expect the unexpected from this innovative leader of design. To order, Dogwear, New York; Town & Country Dogs, London.

Hank Londoner

Bow Blass is the master of ladylike reserve. This nautically inspired suit, *opposite page*, exhibits the economy of line which makes Blass the favorite of ladies who lunch. The navy blazer sports crisp white lapels. The back belt is striped in the same fabric as the middy blouse . . . and is buttoned in gold. The jaunty white pleated skirt completes the silhouette . . . intended to flatter every bitch. To order, Dogwear, New York: Town & Country Dogs, London.

Ruff Lauren evokes the untamed spirit of the West in frontier denims. The time-honored cowboy jacket, *right*, is abbreviated into the back of a streamlined knit dress. The dress can trace its origins to the casual polo shirt—a mixed metaphor that delivers more fashion than the sum of its parts. The colors are true blue and red in celebration of the country which inspired the Lauren look. To order, Dogwear, New York: Town & Country Dogs, London.

Depart from the ordinary . . . Let your imagination take flight in a sophisticated approach to fashion. Well-bred classics, these timeless silhouettes reveal a careful attention to detail never before seen in dog dressing. A delicate balance between proportion and ornamentation . . . Simple shapes rendered sensational by the masters of European design. . . .

The suit. In Red. A bold stroke of genius from **Karl Dogerfeld** for **Kennel**, *opposite*. Tailored to perfection, it features the classic Kennel details—the tweed, the braid, the buttons — the quiet authority to go everywhere and be noticed. Coco would be pleased. . . . Pearls and gold chains by **Kennel**, through Dogwear. To order, Dogwear, New York; Town & Country Dogs, London.

The coatdress, *right*. An unexpected mix of basic and bold from **Christian Diog**. The ladylike lines are shot with gold . . . a flutter of sparkling pleats, punctuated by a coin-buttoned belt. The way to look for daytime or dinner . . . with a distinctive edge to set you apart from the crowd. Pearls from **Van Cleef and Arfpets**, through Dogwear. To order, Dogwear, New York; Town & Country Dogs, London.

Paris/London

NEW DIRECTIONS IN COUTURE

Hank Londoner

Paris/London

Prints charming . . . the innocence of calico and lace, *right*, done as only <u>Laura Afghan</u> can. Delicate lace frames the face and defines a slender waistline. The full gathered skirt skims the floor, evoking the mood of a bygone gentility. Serene and simple, it's a fresh new sensuality for garden parties . . . quiet evenings at home . . . candlelight dinners . . . To order, Dogwear, New York; Town & Country Dogs, London.

Opposite page: Blush pink satin envelops the body in heavy folds. A look befitting a princess, this memorable evening creation by <u>The Edoguelles</u> is inspired by a royal wedding gown. The sweetheart neckline is edged with a ruffle of lace, gently touched with pearls. A wide sash hugs the waist and is caught in a bow. The style is very English . . . and ever so charming. To order, Dogwear, New York; Town & Country Dogs, London.

BLACK TIE AND TAILS
the look for evening

The drama of a special evening. . . . You make an entrance . . . the room stops . . . all eyes watch your every move. . . .

Opposite page: Stun them . . . in the perfect look for evening, an undeniably sexy design that is very, very <u>Yves Saint Bernard</u>. . . . The gold lamé bodice is revealed beneath a gossamer of burgundy chiffon. The fragile cape is frosted with a cobweb of gold embroidery. The bottle-green velvet skirt completes the ensemble, which is simply sensational for the special evening ahead. To order, Dogwear, New York; Town & Country Dogs, London.

Float into the room in a one-shouldered creation from <u>Oscar de la Rawhide</u>, *right*. He understands night glamour in all its subtle implications . . . and his gown will make any dog feel beautiful. Mauve satin is swathed with rose and mauve chiffon, gathered over the bodice and caught at the shoulder in a dramatic jeweled clip. The chiffon spills down from the shoulder to float free with every movement. The sensuous outline evokes the splendor of a Grecian goddess . . . a role anyone would love to assume for the evening. To order, Dogwear, New York; Town & Country Dogs, London.

Hank Londoner

B LACK TIE AND TAILS

Satin and the little black dress. . . . Geoffrey Bone gives us the perfect example of understatement and restraint for evening, *right*. The simple lines are accented with bold strokes of silver . . . a subtle but sensational look for night. To order, Dogwear, New York; Town & Country Dogs, London.

Opposite page: A classical fluted column . . . tiny pleats caught at the waist with baroque golden braid . . . the signature evening silhouette from Mary Muttfadden. Simplicity and opulence combine in an outstanding archetype of evening wear that is softly flirtatious and wholly feminine. A slender reed of crushed berry fabric to wear now and forever. To order, Dogwear, New York; Town & Country Dogs, London.

FURS:
a touch of
L U X E

The temperature drops. Your longing for fur rises. Give in to the urge. . . .

Left: Starkly simple, the Barkglama mink coat from <u>Fendog</u> is everything a coat should be. The clean lines follow the contours of the body for a new fit that is sleek and sexy. A departure from the overpowering shapes of last season, the new line is body conscious and elegant. The stand-up collar is the perfect foil for important jewelry . . . like the gold collar from <u>Bulldogari</u> shown here. To order, Dogwear, New York; Town & Country Dogs, London.

Opposite page: You deserve the best. And this is it. A warm cloud of luxury to keep the cold at bay. A mink coat in Dogday Haze by <u>Barkgrrr Christensen</u>. The dramatic cape collar adds an air of mystery to this extravagant design. A very special coat for a very special dog. Pearls from <u>Van Cleef and Arfpets</u>. To order, Dogwear, New York; Town & Country Dogs, London.

Hank Londoner

Red stitching takes the curves on a black motorcycle jacket, *front*, by <u>Terrier Mugler</u>. The ultimate driving attire for gas station dogs and other road scholars. To order, Dogwear, New York; Town & Country Dogs, London.

Taxicab yellow changes gears, *center*, in a car coat from <u>Claude Mountaindog</u>. The detachable hood, not shown, is optional equipment in a stylish attitude guaranteed to get you where you want to go. To order, Dogwear, New York; Town & Country Dogs, London.

Cruising in a convertible. . . collar, that is . . . by <u>Terrier Mugler</u>, *rear*. Worn down, the black leather collar matches the rest of the jacket for a look of quiet restraint. Flipped up, the collar reveals a lining of plaid, gaining extra fashion mileage. To order, Dogwear, New York; Town & Country Dogs, London.

LEATHERS FOR DOGS *IN THE FAST LANE*

Smart, tough, and built for speed . . . A trio of leather flight jackets takes off down the highway of style.

DOWNHILL RACERS: ski togs for dogs

Take to the slopes in a jump suit that's sleek and functional. Serious skiers and snow bunnies alike choose an outfit that looks and moves well. This jump suit, by <u>Muzzle</u>, combines both criteria with a sense of humor. Imagine, *people* on skis! The levity ends here—sherpa lining and a nylon ciré shell mean no-nonsense warmth and dryness. Complete the look with an angora cowl hood and mirrored wraparound goggles which keep out the elements . . . let in the compliments. To order, Dogwear, New York; Town & Country Dogs, London.

35

BLACK, WHITE, and BOLD!

Strong patterns take charge on dramatic sweaters. Black and white . . . no gray areas here. Designers make a definite statement that is slick on any dog, but especially striking on black and white coats, as shown here. Crisp! A new clarity of design which is seldom seen in dog sweaters . . . a sophisticated look for day or night . . . Black and White. . . .

Opposite page: The shock of white dots on black. <u>Puppy Ellis</u> offers hot dots for all hot dogs! A Dalmation seen in the negative . . . a strong daytime look which can carry you into the night. To order, Dogwear, New York; Town & Country Dogs, London. *Below:* Cheerful and *modern*—a current day harlequin sporting the traditional diamond motif looks freshly new when seen in black and white. <u>Puppy Ellis</u> creates this crisp interpretation for fall. To order, Dogwear, New York; Town & Country Dogs, London.

"Bones are a dog's best friend. . . ." Ruff Lauren delivers a tongue in jowl interpretation of a classic turtleneck design. The graphic quality of black and white makes this sweater fresh and new. To order, Dogwear, New York; Town & Country Dogs, London.

Crystals catch the light and reflect the many facets of your beauty. <u>Bow Blass</u> designs a glamourous evening sweater which is sure to become a favorite. The knit shuns wrinkles and just begs to be packed along for all your flights of fancy. To order, Dogwear, New York; Town & Country Dogs, London.

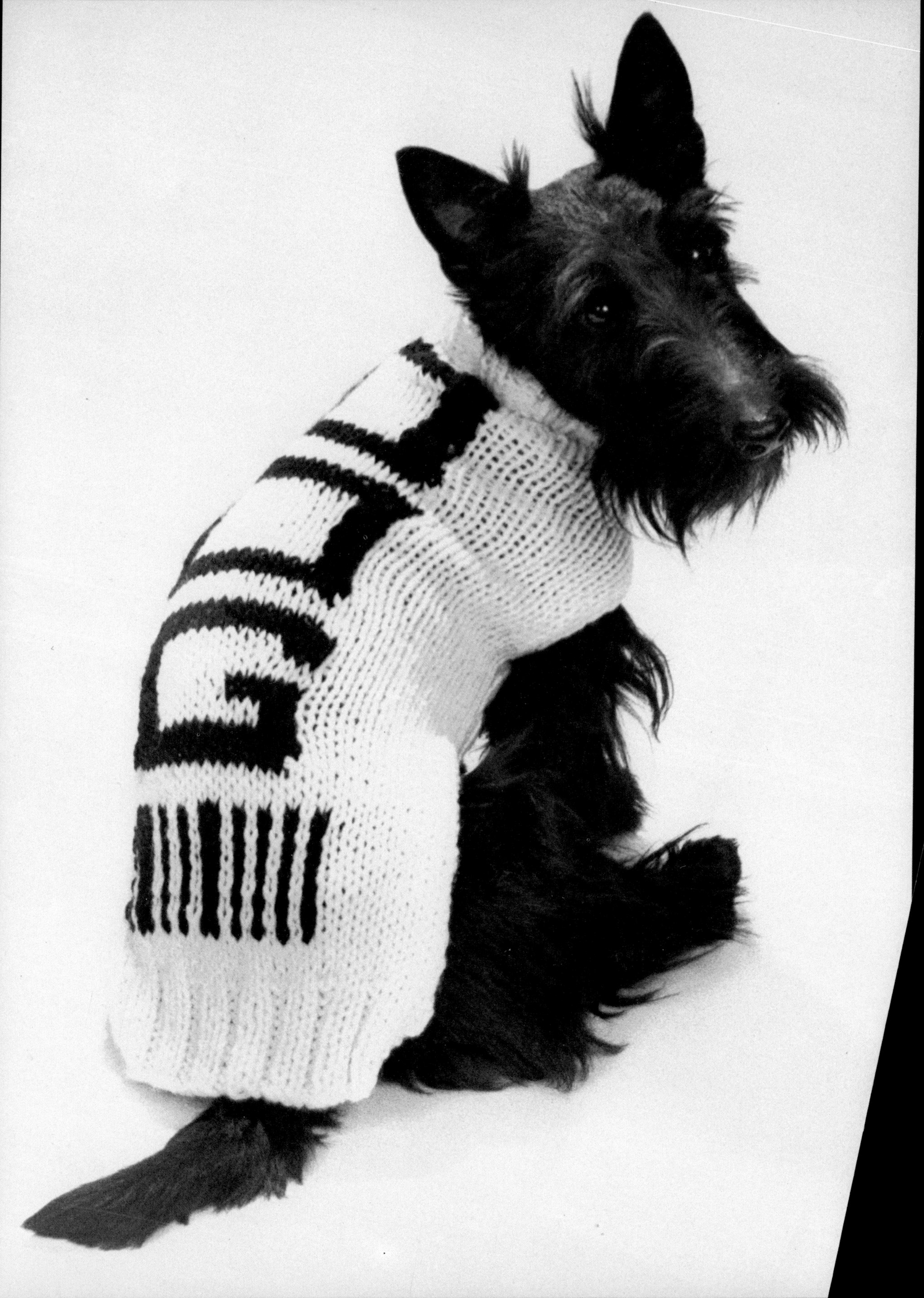

BLACK, WHITE, AND BOLD!

THE WORKOUT: active gear with shape and color

Go for the burn! Colorful workout gear from the Guru of Fitness, <u>Jane Fido</u>, lets you stretch your fashion horizons.

A sparkling example of exercise attire, the pink sweatshirt comes alive with a scattering of rhinestones to reflect your every move. The look packs enough fashion punch to take it from the gym to the streets. To order, Dogwear, New York; Town & Country Dogs, London.

Layers of color can be pulled off or piled on to warm active muscles. Vivid brights of green and gold are only two examples of a rainbow of choices available from <u>Jane Fido Activewear</u> in the basic polo T-shirt and crew-necked sweatshirt. It's a style that pulls its weight in fashion circles. To order, Dogwear, New York; Town & Country Dogs, London.

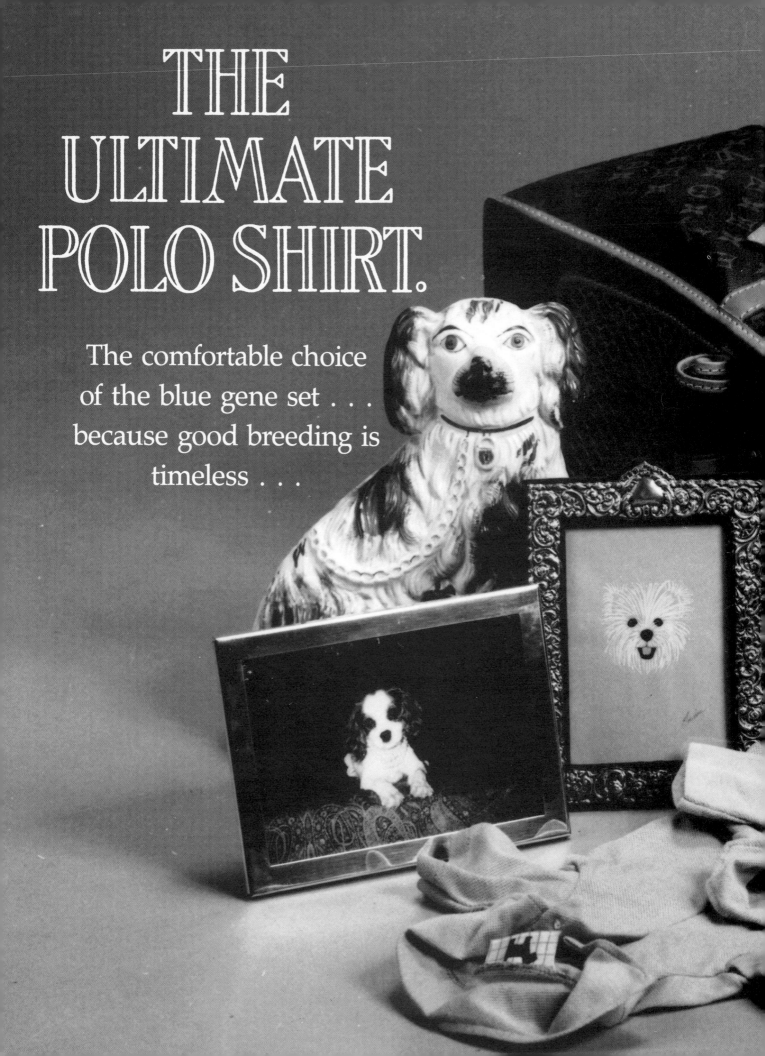

Ruff Lauren for Dogwear

FAUX GEMS

BEAUTIFUL BAUBLES FOR BOW WOW

Pop open the vault to unleash a dazzling collection of jewels for the dog who has *everything*. Pearls, crystals, gold, and silver are fashioned into nostalgic dog collars and modern chokers. Ropes of beads can be the luxurious ties that bind. . . .

From the left, a collection of crystal chokers from Bulldogari, by Dogwear. Necklaces in a variety of colors, textures, and lengths to suit every mood, every fashion, every size. The closure is a miniature dog leash snap, a whimsical reference to the utilitarian dog collars which influenced this very smart look. Silver hearts dangle from a silvery beaded cord, the signature motif of Elsa the Petti. This design and others are available from Rin-Tin-Tiffany & Co., by Dogwear. To order, Dogwear, New York; Town & Country Dogs, London.

Hank Londoner

mENSWEAR

attire for the business animal

The working dog's day is never done. Up early for a jog around the park, the Business Animal must don the uniform of the workaday world before heading down to the office.

Collar and leash sets, *opposite page*, are tailored from the finest traditional woolens—pin stripes, Prince of Wales plaids, hound's-tooth checks, flannels—to build a true dress-for-success wardrobe. The look is classic and equally suitable for corporate dogfights or dinners. Canine Klein for Dogwear. The white button-down collar, *below*, is fashioned from leather to stay clean without expensive trips to the laundry. The variety of four-in-hand and bow ties in conservative foulard prints provides a touch of color to a world of often somber woolens. The leash is tailored from gray pin stripe, the perfect choice for the dog days of business. Ruff Lauren for Dogwear. It can be a dog-eat-dog world out there, but these business-dog looks, from Dogwear, let you get a leg up on the competition. To order, Dogwear, New York; Town & Country Dogs, London.

They say that clothes make the dog, but what better way to personalize your image than with the addition of one of these attractive accents?

Left: Walking the Dogue has never been so glamourous . . . a quartet of collar and lead sets in antique metallic ribbon layered over leather is the perfect choice for a special evening out. The style says well-bred elegance in a quiet way. From Adogfo, by Dogwear. *Opposite page:* Going to the dogs is a pleasure when you can wear collars like these. *Clockwise from top left:* A lacy Pierrot collar set on a velvet band is a demure and innocent look from Ruff Lauren, by Dogwear. An oversized silk taffeta bow is the perfect way to accent a Kennel suit, from Karl Dogerfeld, by Dogwear. A pearl choker on velvet shows your good breeding, from Ruff Lauren, by Dogwear. A rose is a rose . . . especially when it's worn by you. The red leather rose is offset by green snakeskin leaves, from Oscar de la Rawhide, by Dogwear. Silver crystal briolettes form drops on a black velvet collar, from Mary Muttfadden, by Dogwear. Red sequins charge a velvet collar with sparkle, from Bow Blass by Dogwear. Mirrored discs on a velvet band reflect your good taste, from Geoffrey Bone by Dogwear. Metallic ribbon appliquéd over leather is a special look for a special dog, from Koos van der Arfer by Dogwear. To order, Dogwear, New York; Town & Country Dogs, London.

COLORFUL CONTRASTS
collars complete the look

Hank Londoner

PATTERN 761-9356

A COMPLETE WARDROBE

to sew at home

It's a dog's life! The leisure hound is certain to be the center of attention if she steps out in active wear like this from *Ruff Lauren for Dogwear*. The classically styled designer T-shirt and sweatshirt are similar to those available for people, so you can even dress your people in a matching look for those daily outings! The T-shirt, *right*, can be sewn in a variety of knit fabrics—in colors, textures or not—to create a rainbow of summer outfits. The two-button placket collar can be worn down or turned fashionably upward. The sweatshirt, *opposite page*, features raglan sleeves and can be worn alone or layered over the T-shirt, as shown, for a variety of great looks. Colors can match or contrast for more impact. Both shirts are featured in McCall's Crafts Pattern 761-9356, which also includes instructions for a raincoat with a removable hood, and two decorative collars for evening. To order, McCall's Patterns, 230 Park Avenue, New York, New York 10069, (212) 880-2600.

PATTERN 761-9356

PHOTOGRAPHERS IN DOGUE

- FIDO SCAVULLO
- HOUNDMUTT NEWTON
- GRRRICHARD AVEDON
- HUNDT P. HUNDT
- RUNNING PENN
- DEBRUFF TURBERVILLE

Over the years *Dogue* has been recognized as an innovator in the use of photography to depict fashion and beauty in an artful manner. Condog Nast first published *Dogue* in America in 1909, but it was not until the *soignée* Thirties that photography began to overtake the use of paintings and drawings to illustrate the latest styles. *Dogue* has been instrumental in the discovery and development of many canine cameramen whose names are doghousehold words today. The history of photography is rife with names first seen in the pages of this magazine . . . Scavullo, Newton, Avedon, Hundt, Penn, Turberville . . . photographers whose lenses probe the physical and spiritual beauty of the canine form and bring us that much closer to understanding why *dog* spelled backwards is *god*.

- **Fido Scavullo** is the master of play-dead glamour. His pawtraiture of beautiful bitches is legendary. This photograph, *left*, of a young beauty named Millie, is striking in its elegance. What dog wouldn't kill to be captured in this way?

- **Houndmutt Newton** is known for his sinister and sometimes decadent fashion photography, first featured in *Dogue* during the turbulent Sixties. This exquisite photograph, *right*, appeared recently to showcase the work of a talented New York jewelry designer, Philip Zowine. Some people find Houndmutt Newton's work disturbing, but we find this photo in particular to be quite appropriate. The woman *deserves* to be bitten for trying to upstage the beautiful Labrador Retriever, Sally.

PHOTOGRAPHERS IN
DOGUE

• **Grrrichard Avedon** emerged during the Sixties with his fresh approach to fashion photography. Models of earlier years had been captured frozen in static poses, but Grrrichard Avedon caught his models moving freely through space in action. Here, famed English model, Kimberly, *right*, seems to fly through space in a metallic vinyl rain slicker.

• **Hundt P. Hundt** was popular in the late Thirties for his startling use of surrealism. This photograph, *opposite page*, taken in 1939, is a parody of Salvador Doggi's limp-watch wit and features a corset designed by Mainboxer.

PHOTOGRAPHERS IN
DOGUE

• **Running Penn** offers a crisp, clean vision of style. His photographs lack deliberate artifice and are striking in their clarity and simplicity. This stunning example of his work, *left*, appeared as a beauty shot in a recent issue of *Dogue* to illustrate the benefits of a mud masque on canine complexions.

• **Debruff Turberville** is recognized for her hauntingly beautiful photographs of dogs lost in thought in surrealistic surroundings. She creates deliberately soft-focused images which infuse the model with a dreamlike quality. Opulent interiors are often draped with drop cloths for a mood of musty antiquity. The photograph shown on the page opposite is typical of this artist's phantasmagorical work.

D**OGUE'S** LAST WOOF

ON FASHION IN THIS ISSUE

The new dressing options . . . canine clothes that work . . . a return to elegance . . . easy wearable clothes . . . uncomplicated classics for day . . . fantasy and opulence for evening . . . itensify the look with jewelry and collars

This season is marked by a return to elegance in fashion. Dogs are paying more attention to what they wear than ever before. Now that the choices for what to wear have reached epic proportions, there's a new meaning to the phrase "clothes make the dog."

Designer dressing is beginning to make its mark on the Dogwear market. Designers are providing us with a fresh point of view that varies from one to the other, but maintains a unity of mood.

The New York Collection is a clean, wearable group of clothes. Canine Klein delivers uncomplicated shapes in crisp linen. Puppy Ellis goes for the shock of brights in shiny satin. Ruff Lauren gives us a new but nostalgic look at the Old West. Bow Blass

casts his sails for the nautical feeling.

Sweater dressing makes a return. The styles are fresh and uncomplicated, relying upon graphic effects for their interest. The best looks are done by Bow Blass, Canine Klein, Puppy Ellis, Ruff Lauren, and Norma Kanineli.

Workout gear from Jane Fido gives us the way to look for exercise or leisure. These upbeat sweats can take you from gym to home or casual weekends in style.

Evening is the time to put on the dog. Oscar de la Rawhide, Geoffrey Bone, Mary Muttfadden, and Yves Saint Bernard are showing some of the most elegant fashions for evening. Their ensembles combine fantasy and opulence—the way to look when rubbing paws with the Beautiful Dogs.

The foreign influence has become an important force in today's fashion. The masters of European design, including Karl Dogerfeld for Kennel, Yves Saint Bernard, and Christian Diog, combine with newer names in Continental fashion—Terrier Mugler, Claude Mountaindog, Fendog, The Edoguelles. These and others are making new contributions to how we look and what we will wear.

The well-heeled dog can exhibit her good breeding in her selection of fashions from the foreign range for Rover. The average dog can also get her teeth into less costly versions from domestic designers. The choices are endless. Every dog can be well dressed. All that's necessary is the desire to sniff out the best clothes for your own needs.

Woof becomes a Legend most?

Barkglama

BARKGLAMA IS THE LEGENDARY MINK BRED ONLY IN HOLLYWOOD BY THE MINK MEN TO THE STARS

Dream Doghouses
ANIMAL MANORS

Pampered puppies . . . A flick of the paw . . . The gesture *grande* . . . The opinion reasoned. Architects stop and listen:
"Oh, to be in the doghouse now . . . one that features wall-to-wall carpeting in designer colors coordinating with brocade or velvet cushions. Stained glass windows would be nice, but, then, I've always been partial to English Tudor."

Dogs in the know, seeking an architect to combine all their design ideas into the perfect pet palace, were once frustrated in their efforts. But no more. The formation of Animal Manors assures the availability of custom-crafted homes for the well-heeled four-legged set. Animal Manors offers the best of architectural and interior design to the dog with the taste and money to make her dream house become a reality.

Animal Manors, headed by Cannon Garber, employs a team of architects and artists to create the ultimate doghouse for every client. The possibilities are endless. Recent commissions include a French Chateau, *right*, authentic in every detail from the mansard roof to the marble floors and tapestry-covered bed cushions. Other recent projects are equally regal. The English Manor House, *far right, top,* features four extra rooms for your toys, wardrobe, and grooming supplies, or the vacant chambers may be furnished with cushions to accommodate weekend guests. The Swiss Chalet, *far right, bottom,* is the ideal ski cottage for weekends out of town. The Alpine-style stuccoed walls form a nice contrast to the rustic cedar-shingled roof. Balconies look onto snow-filled vistas in season, and, by spring, cheerful window boxes are filled with colorful flowers.
(Continued on page 64.)

The French Chateau, the English Manor House, and the Swiss Chalet — *houses by Animal Manors which can be customized to your specifications.*

James Pipkin

Dream Doghouses

The houses by Animal Manors illustrated in this issue of *Dogue* are stock plans which can be built to any size specifications to accommodate the smallest or largest dog. Colors and details can be personalized to reflect the taste of the owner. But Animal Manors will also accept commissions to custom design a house in any architectural style. Some dogs even choose to live in a miniature version of their human's home, although with all the styling possibilities available, most dogs design a house to reflect their own taste preferences.

Homes by Animal Manors are constructed with the finest materials and display everywhere the mark of first-class craftsmanship. They are weatherproof and are equally suitable for outdoors, integrated into the landscape, or inside a human home, adding a sculptural focal point to any room.

Understandably, these houses are not inexpensive, but satisfied clients tell us that they are worth every dog bone invested. And it's particularly nice knowing that when you acquire an Animal Manor house, your purchase is actually helping other dogs less fortunate than yourself. Animal Manors donates a portion of its income to selected non-profit organizations dedicated to helping and understanding animals.

For further information, contact Cannon Garber at Animal Manors, 462 West 23rd Street, Suite 1, New York, New York 10011, (212) 206-6231. She will be happy to get your construction project on its way—and in no time, we guarantee that *Barkitectural Digest* will be calling you. They'd just love to get their teeth into designs like these!

THE INSCRUTABLE ORIENT

East meets West in a Chinese dog pagoda available from <u>Neiman Marcus</u>, *right, top*. The Texas store that caters to every whim of the rich and famous brings us this Shar-pei's dream come true. Complete down to the Chinese silk brocade bed cushion, this home will unfold the mystery of the East in your own back yard. Available by special order from Neiman Marcus, (800) NEIMANS.

DO-IT-YOURSELF DOGHOUSE

Canines with carpentry skills may wish to try their paw at building their own dream house. Instructions for a simple but elegant do-it-yourself domain are available from the <u>American Plywood Association</u>. For information, write to Maryann Olson, Project Coordinator, American Plywood Association, 7011 South 19th Street, P.O. Box 11700, Tacoma, Washington 98411, or call (206) 565-6600.

ENGLISH COTTAGES

A cottage in the Cotwolds may be your idea of a dream getaway. Bring all the charm and innocence of a simpler life to your own home turf. . . . <u>Country Garden Homes</u>, a company founded by Anthony R. Ely-Johnston, creates beautiful replicas of English country cottages in scaled-down sizes perfect for dogs, *right bottom*. The homes are constructed by skilled craftsmen, using the finest materials and a technique that combines traditionally proven methods paired with modern technology. Miniature latticed windows can be fitted with curtains; wrought-iron latches, hinges, and a front-door knocker add the finishing touches. The thatched roof is handcrafted by a master thatcher in Norfolk reed, the best quality material available. Mr. Ely-Johnston has established a real "cottage industry," and his skills as a craftsman mean that he demands perfection in each house produced. He personally supervises each stage of work from initial client discussions through final installation. He can be contacted at Old South End Farm, Little Odell, Bedford, England; telephone (0234) 720775.

LIVING

It's the end of the day . . . you're dog tired and looking for a place to rest your weary bones . . . Dogue *presents its selection of best beds for the sophisticated sleepy set. . . .*

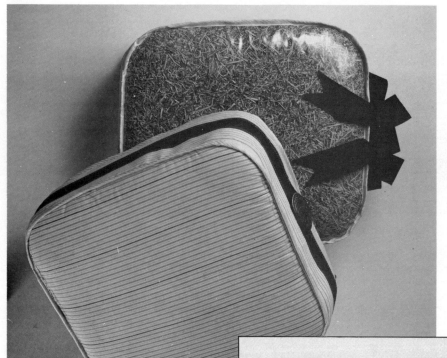

Today's upscale pup wants more than a folded blanket. You want . . . *deserve* . . . the best mattress that money can buy. Classy Neiman Marcus comes to your aid with the richest mattress we've seen. Don't be fooled by the humble striped-ticking covers. *This* cushion is stuffed with over one-million dollars in shredded U.S. currency! You'll rest easy knowing you've got a fortune hidden in your mattress. . . . To order, call Neiman Marcus, (800)-NEIMANS.

Modern Bark-o-loungers from Germany are woven from wicker by the firm of Wilhelm Kuntz. One design features a bunk bed arrangement— room for a guest or a place to go when you're seeking privacy. Another design follows the funky lines of the Fifties— the perfect piece for a pop pad. These beds, and more, are carried by Harrods in London, or may be ordered from the manufacturer: Wilhelm Kuntz, Korb- waren-Industrie, Nachf. Gerhard Neumann, Hauptstrasse 127, 6729 Wörth 3 Schaidt, West Germany. Telephone 06340/8139.

The ultimate choice for the dog who drools over antiques is a custom-crafted bed from William Nichol of Anticus Woodcrafts in Devon, England. Mr. Nichol designs and builds a complete line of fine wooden beds based upon classic furniture designs. His work ranges from an elaborate French confection suitable for Marie Antoinette to a Victorian four-poster, complete with draperies and matching cushion. His beds are not just a thing of beauty—many also feature hidden drawers and compartments in which you can store such valuables as your favorite bones and treats. The bed shown here is representative of the many styles currently available direct from the company or at Harrods in London. To send for a catalog and price list, write to W. Nichol, Anticus Woodcrafts, Coddiford, Cheriton Fitzpaine, Devon, England EX17 4BD.

Decorate your room with a wooden sleigh bed and matching nightstand from Paris. Le Petit Monde du Chien, 14 rue des Bernardins, has designed a sleek bedroom ensemble of rare practicality. The nightstand is fitted with bowls for food and water. You'll never have to make a late-night run to the refrigerator again!

Rugged outdoor-dogs look to the Orvis catalog to satisfy the need for a comfortable and durable place to sleep. The Orvis Dog Nest is one of the best-selling items in the catalog. The removable poly-cotton cover contains a cushion filled with polystyrene beads, making the bed as comfortable as the bean-bag chairs that were popular several years back. The dog nest comes in four sizes, and covers are available in four different patterns. You can order an Orvis catalog by calling (802) 362-1300, or write to Orvis, 10 River Road, Manchester, Vermont 05254.

Critter Comfort is the manufacturer of a heated waterbed for dogs. Besides comfort, the veterinarian-tested bed offers therapeutic value to ill or convalescent dogs. Consisting of a frame, mattress, mattress cover, and heater, the bed is available in three sizes and comes with a one-year guarantee. For information, contact Lori England, president of Critter Comfort, at 129 S. Clinton Street, P.O. Box 504, Manchester, Michigan 48158, (313) 428-7305.

eNTERTAINING

A BARK-B-Q AND A BIRTHDAY BASH

Round up your friends—we're having a Texas Bark-B-Q! *Dogue* has rustled up a hoedown for the pedigreed blue-gene set. Dress as a prairie dog to rough house at the Triple Bone Ranch! The invitations set the mood—cutouts of a hound dog tied with a colorful neckerchief. Bandanas are provided to each guest as the perfect get-up for the afternoon shindig.

Country vittles and Bark-B-Q fare are certain to please fans of Tex-Mex cooking. Dig in to rib bones simmered in hot sauce and chili dogs with plenty of bite. Rhinestone cowdogs will appreciate the fixin's—a bowl of pet chili (see recipe) and crispy pork rind curls. Even urban cowdogs will get their teeth into grilled hot dogs and burgers. As evening settles in, you can gather 'round the Bark-B-Q pit to exchange tall tails and howl at the moon.

Come and get it!

PET CHILI
Chili Dogs/Chili Burgers

(from Fay and Warren Eckstein's *Pet Aerobics,* Henry Holt and Company)

½ pound lean ground beef
1 small onion, chopped
garlic or salt to taste
1 cup tomato juice

Brown ground meat in a frying pan. Remove meat from pan and drain off any excess fat. Sauté onion and add meat and garlic or salt. Add tomato juice and simmer for 15 minutes. Makes 1 to 2 servings, or more for smaller dogs. Serve alone, or as a garnish over grilled hot dogs ("chili dogs"), or hamburgers ("chili burgers").

Texas Bark-B-Q. Whoopee-ti-yi-yo, git along little doggies. . . .

A Birthday Bash for Bowser. . . .
Every dog has his day, so dig
out the candles and . . . party!

Happy birthday, Bowser! Happy birthday, pal. Today's your day . . . so hyper-
ventilate and entertain. The guest list should
include an interesting selection of friends
from all walks of life to provide a stimulating
exchange of growls and gossip. The invitations need not be formal; indeed, details may
be barked over the phone.

Party hats and individual cups of treats
are fun ideas which add to the festivity of
the event. Noisemakers are not usually
necessary. Plan several games to enliven the
afternoon. Pin the Tail on the Doggy is a
perennial favorite.

The food served should be easy—paw
food—to keep an informal mood to the
party. Crisp, munchy treats, like Haute
Canine Fromage Stix (see recipe), are an ideal
choice. The birthday cake makes a bold
decorative statement to reflect the theme of
the party or the taste of the birthday dog.
Our cake is topped with a bone, but other
appropriate motifs include a full dog dish,
a favorite old shoe, or a likeness of the host's
doghouse. You can bake it yourself or enlist
the aid of a canine caterer, like Famous Fido's
Doggie Deli, to provide a custom cake to
order.

Blow out the candles, sing a chorus of
"Happy Birthday," open the presents, and eat
ice cream—this is a party like all the others,
but with an important difference: Once a
year, it's yours. Happy birthday, top
dog . . . and many more to come.

HAUTE CANINE FROMAGE STIX

1 cup whole wheat flour
1 cup all-purpose flour
1⅓ cups cheddar cheese, grated
3 small garlic cloves, crushed
¾ cup soy oil

Blend oil, cheese, and garlic. Add flour
and mix well. Shape into small rolls ½″
in diameter. Slice into 2″ lengths. Chill
on cookie sheet until firm. Bake at 375°
for 10 minutes. Makes about 48 stix.

ENTERTAINING

Puppies' First Christmas

CHRISTMAS EVE VITA LOAF

1 lb. ground beef
1 egg
⅓ cup whole wheat bread crumbs
½ cup chopped onion
1 cup evaporated milk
½ tsp. garlic powder
½ tsp. brewer's yeast
1 tsp. bone meal
½ tsp. wheat germ

1 tsp. honey or molasses

Mix beef, egg, onion, milk, bread crumbs, garlic, yeast, and bone meal. Mold into loaf. Glaze with honey or molasses and sprinkle wheat germ on top. Bake at 350° for 1 hour. Vita Loaf can be refrigerated or frozen for several servings.

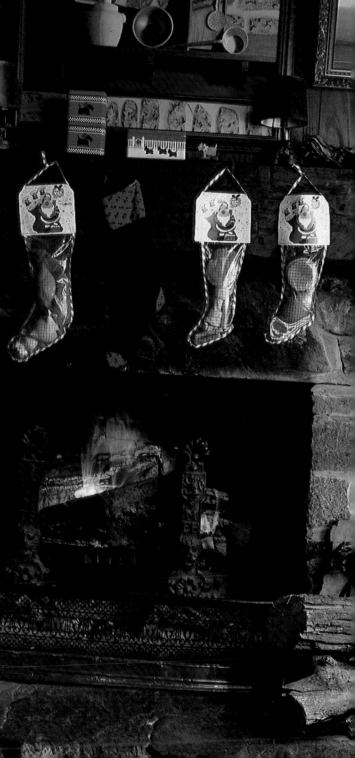

Christmas season marks a time traditionally spent with family and loved ones. The time is made more special when the family has recently expanded with new members. Nubian, a beautiful black Scottie, added eight puppies to her brood on Labor Day, a most appropriate holiday. Since Christmas is a time for children, what greater joy is there than to share a first Christmas with your new family, whether it be an entire litter or a single puppy!

Scotties provide a natural theme for the decor. The family's collection of Scottie figures and decorative objects are used to dress the dining table. Homemade cookies, tied with satin cord, continue the theme as tree ornaments, which are accented by colorful tartan ribbon bows. The figure of an angel, in the guise of a Cavalier King Charles Spaniel, tops the tree, a gift from a favorite aunt (who just happens to be a Cavalier King Charles Spaniel). Gifts are wrapped in Scottie-printed paper, and a large ceramic figure of a Scottie peeks out from under the tree. The tub which contains the roots of the live tree is wrapped in tartan fabric. The tree will be planted after Christmas to commemorate the special and happy event.

The family's home, a 200-year-old stone barn, provides a rustic setting for a holiday gathering of the clan. A beautiful stone fireplace is a warm focal point in the living room and is festooned with Christmas stockings for the puppies.

The festive table is laden with holiday goodies. Treats and biscuits of all shapes and sizes form colorful platters of snacks to be nibbled upon at will. The main course for Christmas Eve dinner is delicious Vita Loaf, a specialty from Famous Fido's Doggie Deli (see recipe). After dinner, the little ones go to bed, to dream about the imminent visit of Saint Nick. The adults help themselves to eggnog and lounge by the fire. The holiday preparations done, it's a dog's life.

BIRD-DOG
GOODMAN

GIORGIO ARFMANI

fOOD IN DOGUE

Haute Canine: Delicacies for the Discriminating Dog

Pampered pets have put their well-heeled paws of approval on a gourmet goodie called Haute Canine (pronounced *oat cahneen).* These luscious biscuits were created by Linda Coffey, a former buyer for Dayton's in Minneapolis, as a treat for her English Sheepdog, Hamel. Needless to say, he could smell a good thing and woofed down the entire first batch. Linda, who also has a nose for success, recognized Hamel's good taste and traded in haute couture for Haute Canine.

As both Linda and Hamel would be the first to agree, Haute Canine biscuits are made with the finest natural ingredients—romano cheese, fresh garlic, eggs, milk, oil, stone-ground whole-wheat flour, and stone-ground corn meal—and each treat is precision-cut with an English biscuit cutter. The result is a dog biscuit different from most other pet snacks on the market, one that contains no additives, chemicals, preservatives, or dyes.

Haute Canine biscuits are sold in a variety of specially-designed packages, including sample packs of two and three biscuits, a 10-ounce signature print doggie bag with a resealable top to guarantee freshness, and a half-gallon unbreakable biscuit jar with a designer-logo label. The latter is topped with a ribbon bow, imprinted with the words, "bone appetit." What more could a fashionable dog want?

What more? Greetings cards, that's what. *Dogue* prefers to think of Haute Canine's clever gift packs as "eating cards," because each one features the two-biscuit sample inside, with messages that range from "Happy Birthday to a true Bone Vivant" to "Season's Greetings and Bone Noël." And of course there are Valentines for the scentimental and beautiful heart-shaped boxes, trimmed with ribbons, and filled with . . . biscuits!

Because Haute Canine products have been selling like hot dogs across the United States and abroad—from gift stores to pet stores, from Neiman Marcus and Macy's to Harrods and more—Linda Coffey has turned her attention to whining and dining and has embarked on the production of a line of fine dog dishes—in bone china—with coordinating place mats. The bowls are cream color with a gold rim and signature logo. They are oven-proof and dishwater safe and come in two sizes. The matching mats wipe clean. The new line has set tongues and tails wagging. Pups are panting to see what Linda is up to next. . . .

For information, contact L. Coffey, Ltd., Haute Canine, 4244 Linden Hills Boulevard, Minneapolis, Minnesota 55410, (612) 925-3209.

FOOD IN DOGUE

How much is that Pup Link in the window? — Famous Fido's Doggie Deli

caters to the four-legged set. . . .

Picture this. The graduation party is a howling success . . . liver paté and cheese logs, followed by a main course of steak and kidney ragout . . . a special graduation cake for dessert and some chocolate chip cookies. And then the toast . . . no champagne, but "a little hair of the dog," a cocktail called Vital 30. The lack of bubbly is no bone of contention for the recent obedience school graduates. After all, they've had to cut corners somewhere so that their catered affair wouldn't go through the woof.

This scenario is typical at Famous Fido's Doggie Deli in Chicago. The firm has catered over 100 parties for dogs at eight dollars per guest. Catering is but one of the functions served by Famous Fido's. Gloria Lissner, the owner, does an excellent restaurant and take-out business as well. "We do not serve dog food," she insists. "We serve food to dogs."

And what food it is! The menu contains appetizers of Tuna Treat, Liver Paté, and Cheese Logs. Main courses feature Shepherd's Pie, Chicken à la Fido, Steak and Kidney Ragout, and Vita Loaf. Desserts include Pup Cakes, Fresh-Baked Cookies, Fido's Famous Cakes, and, finally, Candy Fireplugs. All the foods are made from natural ingredients to enhance bones, teeth, coat, and overall health. Fido's offers a new concept in pet dining, promoting an evening out for a dog and his friends or family.

Famous Fido's has begun to expand its restaurant/take-out concept to areas beyond Chicago. With plans to distribute nationally to pet, gift, and department stores, Ms. Lissner is already manufacturing Famous Fido bakery items—cookies in three flavors (Liver, Cheese, and Liver/Carob Chip, the latter billed as "the world's only canine 'chocolate chip cookie.'") Other new items for broad distribution include Pup Links made of 100% turkey, and other canine treats with such tempting names as Cheese Pretzel, Beef Canine Kisses, Beef Twist, Chicken Croissant, Cheese Bagel, Chicken Bone, Beef Fireplug, and Cheese Sweethearts. Long-term plans include arrangements for deli franchises across the United States. With tongue only slightly in cheek, Ms. Lissner threatens to call the chain "McFido's"!

For more information, contact Famous Fido's Doggie Deli, 1553 West Devon Avenue, Chicago, Illinois 60660, (312) 761-6028 or 29.

T-BONES FOR TWO

Your house is so clean, you could eat off the floor . . . but why bother when you could dress up a delightful dinner for two with personalized placemats from the Orvis catalog? The 18″ x 27″ dinner mats are "set" with napkin, silverware, and bones. Just add a dinner bowl and...come and get it! Order your mat from the Orvis Company, 10 River Road, Manchester, Vermont 05254; (802) 362-1300.

FOOD IN DOGUE

PAWCELAIN POUR VOUS, PHYDEAU
Break out the good dishes. Company is coming for dinner. . . .

Created by <u>Curzon Designs</u>, these bowls, with matching place mats, are the perfect choice for parties or everyday use. The blue-and-white "Good Dog" pattern complements French country decor; the "Woof" pattern has a bright, cheerful appeal. The bowls are dishwasher-safe, and the vinyl mats lick clean. To order, contact Curzon Designs, 561-R Acorn Street, P.O. Box 22, Deer Park, New York 11729; (516) 242-1202.

EAT TO WOOF: Health Foods for Good Nutrition

Several major dog food manufacturers recognize today's concern with health and nutrition and have developed special dog foods which are scientifically formulated to offer a nutritionally complete and balanced diet for all types of canines. Some companies have addressed the needs of dogs with particular medical problems; other companies are concerned with producing all-natural foods with complete nutritional value. Most of these specialized pet foods are not available at the supermarket, but must be obtained at pet supply stores or through your veterinarian.

The Iams Company produces four varieties of dog food, each developed to deliver a sound diet. The four products include *Iams Puppy Food* (for the growing pup until 12 to 18 months of age), *Iams Chunks* and *Iams Mini Chunks* (for all adult dogs—Chunks for large breeds; Mini Chunks, for small and medium)—and *Iams Eukanuba* (a high-stress formula for nursing mothers, growing puppies, working animals, show dogs, and other active pooches) All Iams formulas meet or exceed the nutritional requirements established by the National Research Council of the National Academy of Sciences. To find the address of your nearest Iams dealer, call the company, toll-free, at (800) 525-IAMS; or in Ohio, call (416) 738-0634.

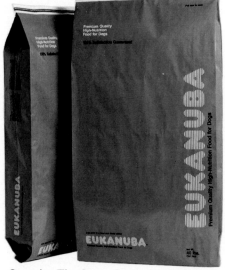

Or write The Iams Company, Box 855, Lewisburg, Ohio 45338.

<u>Science Diet</u> products were formulated by veterinary nutritionists to provide a balance of high-quality nutrients not always found in commercial pet foods and are made by the same people who produce Prescription Diet, the dietary pet foods used by veterinarians as aids in the management of diseases. Science Diet foods restrict ingredients that can aggravate problems such as heart, liver, kidney, and bladder diseases. Because age, temperament, level of activity, and environment create different nutritional needs, there are specific Science Diet foods for each stage of life. *Canine Growth* is for puppies until the age of 12 or 18 months; *Canine Maintenance* is for adult dogs; *Canine Senior* is for older dogs; *Canine Performance* is for adult dogs with higher than average energy requirements; *Maximum Stress Diet* is for guard dogs, sled dogs, and other working animals; and *Mixit* is specially developed for problem eaters. For further information, write to Hill's Pet Products, Inc., Science Diet Customer Service Veterinarian, P.O. Box 148, Topeka, Kansas 66601; or call, toll free, (800) 255-0449.

<u>Cornucopia</u>, veterinarian-created-and-prepared, is a natural food with no added artificial flavorings, colorings, preservatives, sweeteners, or sugars. The products are preserved naturally with vitamins C and E. Megavitamins in the Cornucopia line are guaranteed to be at least 200% of the requirement established by the National Research Council. The four dog food formulas include *Super Start* (for puppies), *Super Life* (for adult dogs to age 7), *Super Senior* (for dogs over 7 years of age), and *Super Stress* (for dogs who are showing, hunting, working, racing, or nursing). For more information, write Veterinary Nutritional Associates, Inc., 229 Wall Street, Huntington, New York 11743, or call the firm's International Pet Health Line at (516) 427-7479.

<u>Hi-Tor</u> dog foods are also all-natural and free of preservatives and additives. They come in three basic formulations, *Hi-Tor All Natural Puppy Food* (for growing pups), *Hi-Tor All Natural Maintenance Diet* (for all adult dogs), and *Hi-Tor All Natural All Beef* (a canned food to be fed alone or mixed with a dry formula for problem eaters). The firm also produces a line of special diets. These include *Intestinal Diet* (a bland diet for dogs with digestive problems), *Reducing Diet* (for the overweight), *Geriatic Diet* (for older dogs), *Puppy Weaning Diet* (for pups from 3 months to one year of age), *Heart Diet* (sodium-restricted for dogs with heart problems), and *Kidney Diet* (low protein and phosphorus for dogs with kidney diseases). For inquiries, contact Triumph Pet Industries, P.O. Box 100, Hillburn, New York 10931; (914) 357-6666.

SPRATT'S . . . to lick the platter clean

Founded in 1862 by James Spratt, <u>Spratt's Patent Limited</u> is the supplier of dog food to Her Majesty the Queen. The Royal Dogs prefer Weetmeet and Flavoured Bones dog biscuits, although the company does manufacture a full range of additional foods. In 1866 James Spratt hired a fourteen-year-old assistant, Charles Cruft, who later founded the prestigious Cruft's Championship Dog Show. Spratt's pet foods are available at most pet shops and supermarkets in England.

ATELIER BARKTEX
PUPPY ELLIS
THE ARF OF MAKING YOUR BED

ARF ART

THE POOCH IN PAWTRAITURE

It's time to sniff about the attic for ancestral portraits. Sporting art, especially those paintings featuring dogs, has been shooting up in value lately. The supply of English art has run nearly dry, especially since American dealers and interior designers have gone barking mad for anything canine!

Dogs have long been featured in ancient art, but it was not until the eighteenth century that artists such as Stubbs, Desportes, and Oudry were commissioned by wealthy patrons to immortalize particular pets. Landseer, a favorite of Queen Victoria and Prince Albert, imparted his portraits of dogs with human expressions and emotions, and inspired countless artists to do the same. Indeed, a whole pack of dog artists from the eighteenth century through the twentieth expressed canines in the most favorable light. Examples of their work are available through antique dealers and art galleries in the United States and Europe.

If you're looking for Arf Art, one antique dealer to consult is Kathie Comerford, president of Kanine Collectibles. Her company specializes in the location and sale of all forms of dog antiques and collectibles and maintains a computerized listing of its stock—catalogued by breed of dog—that is updated daily. For information, contact Kanine Collectibles, Inc., Box 271, 247 Christian Avenue, Stony Brook, New York 11790, (516) 751-2805. Another dealer is J. Garvin Mecking, who stocks a vast selection of antique dog paintings, tapestries, and other unique decorative accessories. His collection is one of the most extensive in the United States. For information, contact J. Garvin Mecking, Inc., 72 East 11th Street, New York, New York 10003, (212) 677-4316.

Jane Millett, *three of whose paintings are seen on this page, works in a realistic style and paints dogs in a nineteenth-century manner. Her portraits show their subjects with complex facial expressions, and she imbues her paintings with a period atmosphere. Recent commissions have included the dogs of the Whitneys and du Ponts, Bob Hope, and Andy Warhol. Jane Millett accepts commissions for portraits and can be reached at 10 Downing Street, Apartment 1R, New York, New York 10014, (212) 924-6263.*

Friedrich Gross *is a modern folk artist from Switzerland, now settled in New York. His work combines the decorative naïve traditions of his homeland with the aggressive and vital rhythms of his adopted city. Gross paints on a variety of surfaces; canvas, wood plaques, country armoires, desks, and building façades have all been graced by his touch. His works exhibit a keen sense of humor, and many of his pieces incorporate images of dogs in their subject matter. The cupboard shown below is representative of his work. Friedrich Gross can be contacted at 478 West Broadway, New York, New York 10012, (212) 473-3057.*

William Wegman *is a photographer who has captured his late dog, Man Ray, in a variety of unusual but visually exciting situations. A selection of his whimsical animal portraits can be seen in a book,* Man's Best Friend *(Harry N. Abrams), but examples of his latest work are available through the Holly Solomon Gallery, 724 Fifth Avenue, New York, New York 10022, (212) 757-7777. That work ranges from original large-format Polaroid photographs to the poster, pictured below, which marked a recent museum exhibit.*

Like William Wegman, **Donald Roller Wilson** *is also represented by the Holly Solomon Gallery. Among Wilson's works is a series of dogs dressed in clothing and painted in a super-realist style (right). Although the artist has had four exhibitions in New York in the past twelve years, his work is better known in his home states of Texas and Arkansas. Wilson's works are both amusing and disturbing, with a complexity of emotion that reaches beneath the surface of the subjects painted.*

79

Jim and Ann Monteith, of **Countryhouse Studios,** *are the premier portrait photographers of dogs in the United States. Their work has been displayed at the Westminster Kennel Club Show in New York, and canine clients come from all over the world to be captured by the Monteiths' camera. The Monteiths can be reached at Countryhouse Studios, R.D. 2, Annville, Pennsylvania 17003, (717) 867-2135.*

ARFART

Duane Hanson *is famous for his realistic figures of people and animals. His works are represented in the Whitney Museum of American Art in New York, which is the home of the life-size sculpture illustrated here. Many other Hanson works feature dogs, and choice examples can be seen in the book* Duane Hanson *(Harry N. Abrams). Hanson's most recent work is available through the O.K. Harris Gallery, 383 West Broadway, New York, New York 10013, (212) 431-3600.*

Julie Evans *is known for her miniature portraits of dogs. She works from photographs of the pet and coordinates the total scope of the project down to the selection of a vintage frame, which she considers integral to the work as a whole. Evans accepts commissions and may be contacted at 203 West 85th Street, Apartment 52, New York, New York 10024, (212) 496-9007.*

Whitney Museum of American Art

Geoffrey Clements   81

DOGS ARE BARKING ABOUT...

HOORAY FOR HOLLYWOOF!

Where do doggy show-biz types hear about the new films or other jobs open for canines in the world of entertainment? They read _Animal Entertainment,_ the _Variety_ of the four-legged theatrical set. _Animal Entertainment_ deals exclusively with all aspects of animals in the entertainment industry—domestic animals, wild animals, circus animals, animals in print ads, commercials, soap operas, prime-time television, and motion pictures. The trade paper also covers celebrities who have pets or are involved with animal welfare, and the trends and story lines being developed behind the scenes by Hollywood producers and writers. The publication features an "industry insider" pull-out section, which focuses on up-to-date animal talent agency listings and producers' animal casting calls. The monthly answer to _Backstage, Showbiz, Variety, The Hollywood Reporter,_ and _Advertising Age, Animal Entertainment_ is for the professional (trainers, handlers, agencies, producers, directors, etc.) as well as the layman. To subscribe, contact Kitty Brown, 1601 Third Avenue, Suite 3CW, New York, New York 10028, (212) 369-2943.

BOOKS ABOUT US

Everyone knows about the American Kennel Club, since 1884 an independent non-profit organization devoted to the advancement and welfare of pure-bred dogs. But how many realize that the AKC also houses a library of more than 15,000 volumes, one of the most complete collections of its kind in the world. Also included in the collection are numerous prints, oil paintings, and other works of art. The public is invited to use the facilities of the AKC library, which is open for reference purposes Mondays through Fridays from 9:00 A.M. to 4:00 P.M. For further information, contact the American Kennel Club at 51 Madison Avenue, New York, New York 10010, (212) 696-8200.

GOOD GRIEF, SNOOPY!

Snoopy, the world's favorite canine, and his sister Belle have been putting on the dog. Dressed to the nines, they've been wearing the stylish creations of over 90 internationally famous couturiers as part of a traveling exhibit, "The Snoopy Fashion Designer Collection."

The designers—among them Karl Lagerfeld, Givenchy, Thierry Mugler, Giorgio Armani, Gianni Versace, Missoni, Krizia, Gucci, Fendi, Kansai Yamamoto, Issey Miyaki, Mary McFadden, and Oscar de la Renta—were presented with a pair of Snoopy and Belle plush dolls and given instructions to outfit them in fashions representative of their work. The results comprise the consummate canine wardrobe, suitable for every occasion—from hiking gear by L. L. Bean and knit ensembles by Missoni to dramatic evening clothes by Oscar de la Renta and bridal attire appropriate for royalty by The Emanuelles.

The exhibit has visited major cities in the United States, Europe, and Asia, including New York, Los Angeles, Chicago, San Francisco, Dallas, Houston, Boston, Atlanta, Miami, Paris, London, Florence, Stuttgart, Sydney, and Tokyo, and plans are being made to take it to other cities as long as this high level of interest continues. If you are interested in learning more, contact June Dutton at Determined Productions, Inc., Box 2150, San Francisco, California 94126, (415) 433-0660.

As Charles M. Schultz, creator of Snoopy and the rest of the _Peanuts_ gang, has said, "Happiness is a warm puppy with a designer wardrobe."

A MUSEUM OF OUR OWN

The Dog Museum of America was founded in 1982 to fulfill a need—to collect, preserve, and exhibit works of art, books, and artifacts on the dog and to provide research facilities and other educational programs. Many other museums and private art collections contain works of art which depict the dog, but none is solely dedicated to canines or so accessible to the public. The Dog Museum mounts approximately four major exhibitions each year at its New York galleries. The themes have been selected to appeal to a diverse audience and have ranged from "The Best of Friends," a history of the dog in art, to "Color Me Dog," an entertaining program designed especially for school children.

By no means limiting its displays to its galleries, the Museum extends its services beyond its four walls by producing a number of traveling exhibits, educational programs, slide and video presentations, lectures and seminars, and books and other publications to bring canine history to dog lovers across America.

To obtain more information about the Dog Museum, its current exhibits, and outside programs, contact The Dog Museum of America, American Kennel Club Foundation, 51 Madison Avenue, New York, New York, 10010, (212) 696-8350.

PUP, WE'RE GONNA MAKE YOU A STAR. . . .

Starstruck dogs in the New York area are pulling together their portfolios at the Star Animal Talent Agency. The founder, Bashkim Dibra, is a professional animal trainer and handler. One of his dogs, Muffin, has been a regular on the popular television soap operas *The Edge of Night* and *One Life to Live,* and was understudy to Benji in the movies starring that loveable pooch. Dibra's animals have appeared in countless films, TV programs, commercials, and print ads. He understands that animals require special training and direction to appear successfully before the camera. Much of the training is similar to obedience schooling, but with a difference—the added strain and distractions provided by crew and equipment present at a professional shoot. Dibra has devised a special course of study to prepare animals for the situations they will encounter at a studio, utilizing photographers, video tape, and film to simulate actual work conditions. Animals who successfully complete the training are provided with a portfolio of the best examples of their work and are eligible to sign up with the Star Animal Talent

Agency Registry, an animal talent agency which will represent its members in obtaining professional bookings. For further information, contact the Star Animal Talent Agency at 3476 Bailey Avenue, Riverdale, New York 10463, (212) 796-4541.

IN THE FOOTSTEPS OF A SAINT

St. Hubert's Giralda is a non-profit animal welfare and educational center. It was founded in 1939 by Geraldine Rockefeller Dodge, the prominent heiress, socialite, philanthropist, art collector, and dog lover. Her residence in Manhattan was the last of the private houses on Fifth Avenue, and her mansion in Madison, New Jersey, Giralda Farms, was filled with art treasures collected over fifty years. The majority of her collections was sold after her death in 1973, but a portion of Mrs. Dodge's extensive collection of animal art is on permanent display at the St. Hubert's Giralda Gallery, which is open to the public.

St. Hubert is the patron saint of animals, but especially dogs. The center was named in his honor and was the first animal shelter in New Jersey to receive accreditation by the Humane Society of the United States. It is regarded as one of the nation's leaders in animal shelter practices and procedures. The center maintains a shelter for the care and placement of stray animals, an educational program to enlighten the community about animal welfare, a pet therapy program which services eighteen neighboring nursing homes, and the art gallery and library.

Of particular interest to readers of *Dogue* is the fact that St. Hubert's has issued a series of limited edition prints of several art works from Mrs. Dodge's collection. The prints cost $30 each, and the proceeds benefit the center. For further information about the prints or about St. Hubert's Giralda, contact the center at 575 Woodland Avenue, Madison, New Jersey 07940, (201) 377-8877 (the education center) or (201) 377-2295 (the animal shelter).

PUNK POOCH

Lynda Barry, the irreverent Seattle artist, creates a monthly comic strip, "True Romance," for Esquire magazine, and her work also appears in newspapers throughout the United States. Barry's two books, *Girls and Boys* and *Big Ideas,* are compilations of her zany but trenchant work, a radical approach to sex, party habits, nutrition, appearance, love, aging, and other problems of the day. She also turns her sharp pen to the canine world with her extraordinary poster, "Poodle with a Mohawk." The 22¾" x 35" poster, shown here greatly reduced, can be ordered directly from the publisher and costs $4; the books cost $5.95 each. Contact The Real Comet Press, 932 18th Avenue East, Seattle, Washington 98112, (206) 328-1801. They may also be available at your local bookstore.

He knew what people thought of his kind: "High Strung." Spoiled Rotten." French." But in the next 24 hours, He's going change all that....

He's SMALL.

He's BLACK.

He's mad as HELL.

HE'S...

POODLE with a MOHAWK

"you'll never call him FiFi again"!

A UNIVERSAL ARTISTS RELEASE · Coming soon
STARRING LYNDA BARRY AND "BOB" © 1982

DOGS ARE BARKING ABOUT...

The Hottest New Videocassette Around...

ARF!™

At Last—Video For Your Dog! (and you)

Yes, TV is going to the dogs. And your dog will love it! "Arf" is all kinds of unadulterated (and some adulterated) dogs. Big barkers and little yippers. Beauties and beasts. Pedigreed and nature's own.

Best of all, it's just for dogs. Think about it. Do you often treat your dog like a dog? When's the last time he got to have his friends over? When's the last time he got to watch what he wanted to watch on TV?

Now, with his own personal "Arf" videocassette, your dog won't have to wait for those rare TV shows that appeal to his interests. Now he can have his very own program . . . one that will not only entertain him, but will speak to him in a language he can understand.

"Arf" is also the perfect gift for your dog-loving friends; they'll say it's the doggonedest thing they've ever seen!

It's canine cinema at its best!

For sale only $14⁹⁵

H-E-E-E-E-E-R-E-'S PUPPY!

Tired of flipping the channles and finding only people on your T.V.? You deserve programming directed at your elevated tastes and areas of interest, shows to hold your attention. Tune in, then, to WDOG-TV, brought to you courtesy of a new video tape called, appropriately, "Arf! Video for Your Dog." Kartes Video Communications makes the half-hour tape available in both VHS and Beta formats. The programs include a game show ("Boners"), an exercise class ("Fitness with Fifi"), a musical show ("Bark Along with Mitch"), and even the Miss Canine America beauty contest. Producer Marlene Lambert has thoughtfully added subtitles to the barking sound track in case any people happen to tune in. The video tape sells for under $15 and can be ordered directly from Kartes Video Communications by phoning, toll free, (800) 582-2000.

ROCK 'N ROLL OVER

Hot dogs are bopping to the sounds of the newest rock sensation, The Mutts. Digger and Woodie, Jack Russell Terriers, have recorded a 12-inch extended play record for Warner Bros. Side A is *Underdog;* side B is *Atomic Dog.* The sound is rap and rock. The Mutts' manager, Niall Rodgers, who also directs Madonna's career, created the group's new sound by using a synclavier (a musical synthesizer) to translate the dogs' barks into a variety of different sounds and rhythms. The proceeds of the record will be donated to New York's Animal Medical Center. Watch for the platter's release soon. . . .

DATELINE: DOGVILLE

A.P. (Associated Press) and U.P.I. (United Press International) provide newspapers with up-to-the-minute news about people. U.P.P. (United Pet Press) is the equivalent wire service for dogs (and other animals). Through an exclusive network of skilled professionals in all areas of the animal world—veterinarians, animal behaviorists, breeders, trainers and handlers, nutritionists, pet-facilitated therapists, psychics, religious leaders, farmers, humane society workers, and celebrities (both two- and four-legged)—and from New York to Los Angeles to London—U.P.P. channels animal information, in easy-to-understand editorial copy, to the general print and broadcasting media. To subscribe to United Pet Press, contact Kitty Brown at 1601 Third Avenue, Suite 3CW, New York, New York 10028, (212) 369-2943.

DEARLY DEPARTED

Some people choose to bury their departed pet friends in the yard. Others seek a more grand and timeless setting. For the latter, *Dogue* recommends consulting a reputable pet cemetery. There are more than 500 in the United States alone.

The nation's oldest and most respected pet burial ground is the Hartsdale Canine Cemetery in Hartsdale, New York. Founded in 1896, it is a beautiful and fascinating place to visit. (Arrangements can be made through the cemetery office, 75 North Central Park Avenue, Hartsdale, New York 10530, (914) 949-2583).

A lovely and unusual book, *The Peaceable Kingdom in Hartsdale* by Malcolm D. Kriger, records the history of this famous cemetery and explores the stories of some of the pets who rest there. Beautifully illustrated, and with a warm and personal text, the book is available by mail order for $20 plus $1.50 for postage and handling per copy. Requests may be mailed to Rosywick Press, 175 West 12th Street, New York, New York 10011.

DEDICATED
TO THE MEMORY OF
THE WAR DOG
ERECTED BY PUBLIC CONTRIBUTION
BY DOG LOVERS. TO MAN'S MOST
FAITHFUL FRIEND. FOR THE VALIANT
SERVICES RENDERED IN THE
WORLD WAR
1914 — 1918

STICK 'EM UP!

Puppies, like children everywhere, are not immune to the latest craze. This week's fad is the collecting of colorful stickers to be pasted into scrapbooks. Among the many themes are "Outfit a Pooch," "Design a Dog," and "Puppy Trivia." These stickers and others are available at local stationery and paper goods stores, or contact the manufacturer, Sandylion Sticker Design, 340 Alden Road, Markham, Ontario, Canada L3R 4C1.

EAT ANY GOOD BOOKS LATELY?

Tired of chewing over the same old shaggy dog stories? Why not try such classic puppy story books as *Circus Dogs, Doggie Pranks,* and *Bow Wow Stories* — reproductions of antique originals from the turn of the century. They may be purchased at local museum shops and toy or stationery stores, or ordered directly from the publisher, B. Shackman & Co., Inc., 85 Fifth Avenue, New York, New York 10003, (212) 989-5162.

BITING SATIRE

" 'Woof, Woof' slurps a happy Rover as he sinks his slobbering jowls into a world leader," reads the copy on the package containing the latest objects of "biting satire" from England's great television program *Spitting Image*. Pet Hates are the chew toys inspired by the hit show, cartoon busts of President Ronald Reagan and Prime Minister Margaret Thatcher, aka the "two fab flavors—Meaty Maggie and Rancid Ronnie"! The toys are safe and non-toxic and recommended to help you "articulate your political leanings by giving you a top politician to chew to death." Other world leaders will be offered soon. Pet Hates are manufactured in England by Armitage Brothers, Nottingham.

tRAVEL NOW

FASHION DOGMA: The Best Places to Shop in London, Paris, and New York

Where do the Top Dogs shop when visiting the world's major cities? Fashion hounds on the social circuit make a point of stepping into their favorite stores to see what's new and to pick up a few chic items unavailable at home. We've culled the favorite haunts of several jet-set dogs to share with you.

LONDON is the home of Town & Country Dogs in the fashionable Sloane Street district. Luxurious shops abound, and this one is no exception. Christopher Grievson, proprietor, is the second generation of his family to cater to the needs of the world's finest dogs. He has been responsible for matching many special dogs with special human companions. Princess Grace, Charles de Gaulle, Eva Peron, the Aga Khan, Elizabeth Taylor, Lauren Bacall, Cary Grant, Elton John, Sir John Gielgud, Zsa Zsa Gabor, and Jackie

Onassis are only a sampling of the many celebrities selected to live with Town-&-Country-bred dogs.

Here a dog can select from a variety of offerings. Custom-made "dog nests" may be covered in any fabric supplied by the customer to guarantee coordination with the room decor at home. Woolen hand-knit sweaters keep company with hand-braided leather collars and leashes. The leather goods are made by special arrangement with the harness makers who supply the Royal Stables, and they are of the finest quality. The shop also houses an excellent grooming salon which uses a line of shampoos, conditioners, and styling sprays that have been developed exclusively for Town & Country. These grooming aids are also available to customers for use at home. For further information, contact Town & Country Dogs, 35-B Sloane Street, London SWI, (01) 730-5792.

Harrods is a London shopping tradition. The buyer for the pet department, Rita Stratta, is known for her keen eye in selecting the finest products. The well-stocked department carries a full assortment of beds in wicker and cushioned fabric. Coats and sweaters are plentiful and in abundant variety. One item of special interest to the globe-hopping dog is the Pet Passport, with pages to be filled in with your vital statistics so

you'll be guaranteed a high level of care should you ever travel apart from your human companions. A Dry-Sac is a bunting made of toweling to keep you warm and dry after a swim. Another alternative is the Harrods Pet Department signature towel, sure to be a thoughtful gift for the dogs back home. For more information, contact Harrods Knightsbridge, London SWI, (01) 730-1234.

PARIS is the favorite fashion stop for many smart pets. It is here that most any fashion fantasy can be realized. Le Petit Monde du Chien features some of the most extravagant offerings. A dog bound for skiing in Gstaad can find a nylon ciré snowsuit lined in fake fur. A cowl-neck hood, muffler scarf, and leg warmers complete the look. A distressed leather flight jacket is faced with real sheepskin for warmth and style. Hand-knit sweaters in a rainbow of colors are a cloud-like confection when made of the softest angora. Travel bags will carry the needs of dogs of any size (as well as the dog himself). The bags are available in fabrics and leathers, with patterns to please any taste. One specialty of the house is a tote bag which opens to form a bed for a quick nap on the go, or in a stylish restaurant (where many of these bags are almost made to be seen). Le Petit Monde du Chien was featured in a fashion show on French television, and it is easy to see why. For information, contact Le Petit Monde du Chien, 14 rue des Bernardins, Paris 75005, (1) 633-8959.

Aux Etats-Unis is an old-guard luggage and leather-goods store (it pre-dates Louis Vuitton). The back room houses an emporium devoted to dogs. Our favorite items are the two-tone collar and leash sets with angora sweaters to match. Some pampered pedigrees have even ordered matching belts and bracelets for their people! Aux Etats-Unis will make these, and other canine classics, to order in any color and size. They can be ready in a week or more at Aux Etats-Unis, 229 rue St. Honoré, Paris 1er, (1) 260-7395.

Goyard is located up the *rue* from Aux Etats-Unis. It, too, is an old-line leather emporium. Goyard can fit you with black tie in a wing-tip collar with matching leash. Special handmade blankets depict every dog breed in a handsome appliqué. Goyard will also make up collars to order in any color or style you choose. For details, contact Goyard, 223 rue St. Honoré, Paris 1er, (1) 260-5704.

Saillard is a store whose main specialty is hunting equipment, but many an elegant dog has left the premises in one of the firm's sporty Harris tweed coats. Rugged hand-crafted collars and leashes in rich leather with metal accents are the signature look. Martha Philipson, Paloma Picasso's dog, shops here exclusively. Contact Saillard at 19 rue Danielle Casanova, Paris 1er, (1) 261-3016.

NEW YORK is a shopper's paradise. Savvy dogs mourn the demise of Saks Fifth Avenue's well-stocked pet department, but other fashionable establishments have risen in its place. Macy's pet department carries everything from canine couture to tasty treats for the chow hound! Vince Rienti, the buyer for the department, brings in only the newest and best items. Macy's is an important outlet for fashions by Dogwear. This new design line has been the talk of *Dogwear Daily*. Hand-knit woolen sweaters by Puppy Ellis, Canine Klein, and Ruff Lauren are among the best we've seen. Some *people* have even been spotted wearing versions of these exclusive fashions. The Ruff Lauren polo shirt can be worn with the signature sweatshirt—both available in lots of bright and soft colors. A white leather button-down collar with a woolen pin-stripe leash can be worn with your choice of blue four-in-hand or berry bow tie, a fashion must for the business animal! Faux gems by Bulldogari are the rage for evening. A more classic look is the pearl choker or lace Pierrot collar. Macy's also carries a full line of gourmet foods and other necessities. Contact Macy's, Herald Square, New York, New York 10003, (212) 560-4261.

Karen's for People and Pets is another place to find fashions for your people, fashions which reflect your own style preferences. Karen Thompson has a knack for selecting the newest of the new. Large jewels can be had for your people as well as yourself. Heard about people with money to burn? Well, at Karen's, pets can find money to *chew*. That's right, an exclusive chew toy resembles a stack of large bills. It's sure to be a favorite with the upwardly mobile.

Shopping at the stores listed here is sure to be fun, but costly. Our final word of advice would be to bring your master's card. Don't leave home without it.

It can be reached easily by car or bus. Buses run daily from the Victoria Coach Station in London.

Oh, Taxi! Taxi! New York's Critter Car takes you where you want to go . . . London's Move-a-Pet gets you going abroad . . .

Dogs in London and New York are finding it easier to hail cabs these days. Until recently, most cabbies would not respond to a raised paw or a bark which sounded suspiciously like "taxi!" Many other car services were reluctant to answer calls from customers of the canine persuasion. And then the Critter Car cruised into view.

The Critter Car was created by Barbara Meyers out of necessity. She was herself recovering from orthopedic surgery when her beloved friend, Duke, a German Shepherd, was stricken with terminal cancer. Meyers was unable to drive Duke to the animal hospital to receive treatment, and she discovered that taxi drivers were unwilling to transport the pair to their frequent medical appointments. Meyers had to depend upon the kindness of a friend, who agreed to drive the two of them to the hospital as often as was necessary. Shortly after Duke died, Meyers founded the Critter Car establishment, a taxi service for animals.

The Critter Car operates two cars, with specially trained drivers who are understanding of the needs of their special passengers. The cars respond to the call of *any* animal who can travel comfortably in an automobile, not only dogs. The service operates daily from 8 A.M. to 8 P.M., although emergency calls are answered at all hours. Reservations may be made in advance, at no extra charge, and animals can travel alone or with their people. Although located in Brooklyn, the Critter Car will send cars to pick up or deliver dogs in other boroughs of New York or in nearby states; the rate charged is based on mileage. And you needn't be in need of a vet to use the service. The Critter Car will take you almost anywhere—to your groomer, hotels, parks, the airport, just plain visiting,

or really anywhere you choose to go! You can hail a Critter Car by calling (718) 377-2929, or contact The Critter Car, Inc., 5419 Fillmore Avenue, Brooklyn, New York 11234.

Move-a-Pet Ltd. provides a similar service. In fact, Move-a-Pet is the European paw of the business, servicing London, all of England, and all of Europe. Reservations for European travel can be made through Move-a-Pet Ltd., 422-A Upper Richmond Road West, East Sheen SW 14, London. Call (1) 878-5122 and speak to Don Milton to plan your next European trip.

Collar your human companion to visit Leeds Castle, near London . . .

Leeds Castle maintains a well-known Dog Collar Museum in its gatehouse. This display is quite extensive and ranges from medieval spiked collars, which protected hunting dogs from bears and wolves, to ornate silver collars of the last century. Leeds Castle is located in Maidstone, Kent, 40 miles from London, just off the M20 motorway.

Puppy Pleasures: Hotels for Hounds

The travel brochure resembles so many others, with photos of happy vacationers surrounded by luggage, guests checking in at the front desk, an attractive restaurant, a typical hotel room. Yet, this brochure is strangely different from the others because it describes "a hotel so exclusive it doesn't accept *people*"! The brochure is for The Montrose Pet Hotel, the newest luxury pet hotel in New York City. With three other locations in Maryland, Virginia, and Georgia, the Montrose Hotels may be the fastest growing chain of pet hotels in the industry.

The Montrose Pet Hotels are unique in that they are patterned after a "people hotel." Guests check in at a front desk in a well-appointed lobby. Comfortable chairs, plants, and even a well-stocked boutique for grooming aids, treats, attire, and other souvenirs set the tone for this well-designed facility. Soothing music is piped into the lobby and all of the guests' rooms. Check-in is accomplished at a front desk. Behind the desk are pigeonholes which correspond to each of the guests' rooms. On any given day some of these boxes contain mail and postcards sent to the guest from his vacationing family. The hotel staff sees that these letters are read to the dog, and some lucky ones are even treated with long-distance phone calls from absent family members who miss the sound of Fido's voice!

Yet all of the frills described above do not overshadow the fact that this is a professional operation engaged in the quality care of dogs. The hotel, unlike others in the industry, is open seven days a week, with extended hours on weekends to accommodate the hectic schedules of travelers. No advance

tRAVEL

Hotels for Hounds
(Continued from page 87)

reservations are required, except for convenience during the peak holiday seasons.

The hotel even provides a pet taxi service to pick you up and deliver you home for a small additional charge.

Guests are housed in individual rooms, the sole exception being two or more dogs in the same family who may prefer rooming together at a small discount. The facility is an indoor one, including the exercise runs, so that a climate-controlled environment can be provided. This assures you of exercise on even the hottest, coldest, or wettest of days.

The hotel serves quality brands of canned, dry, or moist packaged food; however, finicky Fidos can be served any special diet if it is provided by the owner. Medication will be administered, and hygiene is maintained through the use of disposable feeding bowls—"a fresh table setting at every meal!"

The Montrose Pet Hotels even maintain a grooming salon on the premises. You can be treated to a shampoo and trim before leaving for home and can arrive at your door all pampered and pretty.

The hotel subscribes to a high level of health and safety standards. It maintains 24-hour security seven days a week, is completely fireproof, soundproof, and screened against insects of all types. All rooms are cleaned and disinfected daily and no guest can check in without a certified clean bill of health from his veterinarian. In the case of an emergency, your own doctor is contacted, and, if not available, the hotel can reach its own veterinarians who are on call 24-hours a day. Owner Donald Mensh is proud of Montrose's high standards, and he has good reason to be. He is a charter member of the American Boarding Kennels Association (ABKA), the professional organization of kennel operators founded in 1977.

The group was founded to set professional standards for the industry and to provide a means of education and exchange of information for its members. The ABKA, with a membership of over 1,000 kennels throughout the U.S. and Canada, has outlined a code of ethics and standards by which its members must abide. The organization conducts seminars, conventions, and regional meetings to exchange ideas, and its members are constantly informed of new developments in pet care through its certification program and publications. James Krack, the Executive Director of the ABKA, has also written a brochure called "How to Select a Boarding Kennel," which outlines what things you should consider when choosing a kennel for a vacation. The brochure lists the professional standards for a well-run kennel and provides a list of questions that should be answered by the kennel before you entrust yourself to its care. The booklet also includes the current membership roster of the ABKA, those kennels which fulfill the standards recommended in the brochure. Names, addresses, and phone numbers are provided in this listing, which is arrranged alphabetically by state and city for your convenience in selecting an appropriate kennel. The booklet is available for $1.00 per copy from The American Boarding Kennel Association, 311 North Union, Colorado Springs, Colorado 80909. Mr. Krack can be reached at (303) 635-7082 and will be happy to answer any of your questions concerning the selection of a quality boarding kennel for your next holiday.

The Montrose Pet Hotel is only one of many quality facilities recommended by the ABKA. Another fine hotel in the New York area is The Willow Pet Hotel located in Deer Park, New York. Jack Rosensweig, the owner, is not only a founding member of the ABKA, but he has been awarded the coveted Certified Kennel Operator (CKO) plaque by the organization for his exceptionally high standards. Mr. Rosensweig offers many of the same services as the other hotels mentioned, but he also provides for supplementary playtime for those who may miss the daily human interaction while their family is away. In addition, health insurance is available to protect you and your family from unforseen expenses in the case of an accident or sudden illness. Mr. Rosensweig also maintains a pet travel agency on the premises, so that you can arrange for your next trip.

Another special pet resort is Kennelwood Village in St. Louis, Missouri. This complex is run by Alan Jones. The facility can provide grooming and even training classes during your stay. Kennelwood is very active in local pubic service and charity work. Judy Strickland, the director of training, has conducted a local radio show and a weekly seminar to keep local dogs and other animal lovers aware of new developments in pet care. Kennelwood has also arranged for annual dog beauty contests to benefit local charities, the latest one conducted for the local humane society. At Christmas the resort offers to take your photo with Santa, and again the proceeds go to local charity groups.

Another innovation is "Camp Kennelwood," a summer program of rest and recreation for you and your *owners*, because everyone deserves some time away, even humans.

Hollywood dogs get the star treatment at the Almont Kennels in Los Angeles, California. Cathi Helfer's kennel has been written up in *Los Angeles* Magazine and provides such innovations as rooms with blankets, a summer camp, and even two "cookie times" each day to pamper its pet personalities.

Jet-set pets usually plan a stop at the ASPCA Animalport at New York's Kennedy International Airport. Animalport is the western hemisphere's oldest and largest kennel. In the last twenty-five years it has catered to over one-million satisfied animal customers. Animalport is open 24 hours a day, seven days a week to make it convenient for travelers who arrive or leave at any hour. It provides a pick-up and delivery service to any of the terminals at JFK Airport, and, staff permitting, can arrange for service to LaGuardia Airport as well. This facility is particularly convenient for travelers into or out of New York City. Passengers with a layover between flights can come to the Animalport for rest, exercise, or feedings between flights. It's also the perfect place for a dog to spend an overnight stopover. No reservations are required, but it is wise to call in advance, particularly during peak vacation periods.

When it comes to vacation time, you'll find that you have as many resort options as your human friends do . . . perhaps more, because while many people hotels will welcome dogs, animal hotels, like those mentioned here, are more selective: They won't accept people!

PET HOTEL DIRECTORY:

The Montrose Pet Hotel
312 East 95th Street
New York, New York 10128
(212) 831-2900
　other locations:
Rockville, Maryland . (301) 770-5446
Fairfax, Virginia ...... (703) 425-5000
Atlanta, Georgia ..... (404) 977-2000

The Willow Pet Hotel
1926 Deer Park Avenue
Deer Park, New York 11729
(516) 667-8924

Kennelwood Village
755 New Ballas Road South
St. Louis, Missouri 63141
(314) 872-7007

Almont Kennels
632 N. Almont Drive
Los Angeles, California 90069
(213) 274-0829

ASPCA Animalport
Air Cargo Center
Building 189
Kennedy International Airport
Jamaica, New York 11430
(212) 656-6042

Fido's Flights of Fancy Arranged by a Travel Agent for Pets

Dogs on the go may now arrange their flights of fancy and other journeys through a number of animal travel agencies located throughout the United States. One of these is The Animal Travel Agency at The Willow Pet Hotel in Deer Park, New York. The agency was founded by Jack Rosensweig, the owner of The Willow Pet Hotel, when he perceived the need for someone to cater to the travel requirements of jet-set pets. Most regular travel agencies were not capable of providing the specialized services necessary to arrange for the safe and comfortable transportation of travelers with tails. Mr. Rosensweig and his staff have carefully researched the travel regulations for each of the states and for all foreign countries. They know the available means of transportation to these areas and the places that will happily house you upon arrival at your destination.

The travel agency is a member of IPATA, the Independent Pet and Animal Transport Association, and is an Intermediary Handler registered by the Department of Agriculture. Mr. Rosensweig's company is retained by Fortune 500 companies to arrange transportation and boarding for dogs who accompany relocating and traveling executives. The agency is also contacted by many dogs anxious to have their human friends accompany them on a trip within the United States or abroad.

Mr. Rosensweig can advise you on what vaccinations and certificates are necessary for travel to a different state or country. The agency will make arrangements for every facet of your trip, including a veterinarian to examine, vaccinate, and certify you for travel; obtain tickets for passage; arrange transportation from your home to and from the airport or dock; provide the necessary traveling container for your comfort; and reserve space in a hotel or motel room for your human companions. The agency can also be called upon to provide boarding for you at a local pet hotel if you prefer accommodations separate from your people. (We

all need a little privacy now and then, and separate vacations are sometimes best. . . .) For further information, contact The Animal Travel Agency at The Willow Pet Hotel, 1926 Deer Park Avenue, Deer Park, New York 11729, (516) 667-8586. Jack Rosensweig and his staff will be happy to plan your next trip, or they will suggest an animal travel agency in your area which will be similarly qualified to make the necessary arrangements.

Another travel agency to consider is Canine Carriers, the only Interstate Commerce Commission-licensed carrier of pets in the United States. One telephone call to its toll-free number ensures you of a trouble-free trip to your final destination anywhere in the United States . . . or world. Canine Carrier's president, John Hollywood, assures a comfortable pick-up, in heated or air-conditioned vehicles, from anywhere in the United States, providing all health certificates and other travel documents along the way. Your trip will be carefree, and it can be charged to American Express, Visa, or Mastercard. To receive a free brochure which explains all of Canine Carriers' services in detail, or to book a trip, call (800) 243-9105. In Connecticut, dial (203) 655-7295. The company will be happy to answer all questions and plan your next trip. Bon Voyage, Bow Wow!

Unleash Your Energy at The Doggery Animal Center Health Spas

Pudgy pups go for the burn at an exclusive health spa in L.A. Tinseltown's preoccupation with health and beauty extends to the four-legged set, and now dogs can work out with the pets of Zsa Zsa Gabor, Tina Sinatra, Henry Winkler, and Mel Brooks. These lucky dogs, and others, are members of The Doggery Animal Center.

The Doggery program begins with a con-sultation on nutrition, followed by a growling workout on the jogging exerciser. This version of a treadmill was designed with dogs in mind. The three speeds—walk, trot, and run—increase stamina and have cardiovascular benefits. A fifteen-minute walk equals once around the block in a safe place, free from traffic and potholes.

Lap dogs can take a quick dip in the 6 foot

(Continued on page 90)

Going in style . . .
Tony travel trappings . . .
Designer luggage and
more. . . .

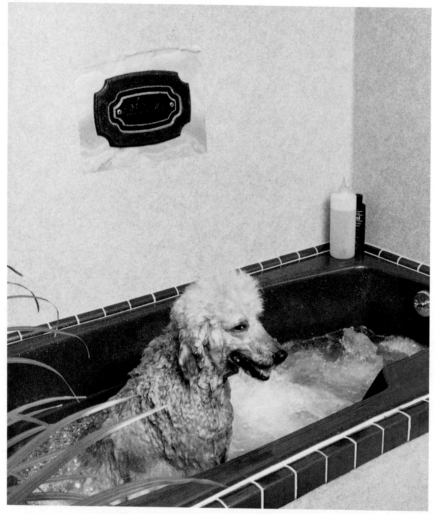

Jet-set pets and other savvy travelers have a way of telegraphing their social status. Whether they're traveling on the show or party circuit, these dogs move in well-bred circles and stay with their own class. Dogs in the know understand that every detail is a reflection of their character and lifestyle, that only the best will do. These pups turn to venerable names when choosing the luggage that will carry them in fashion and comfort.

Louis Vuitton of Paris has been manufacturing luggage since 1854. The brown bags punctuated with the now familiar "LV" logo are almost a fixture at every fine hotel or travel conveyance. The luggage is known for its good looks and durability, and it is chosen by many well-heeled travelers. Doggie needs have not been neglected. Louis Vuitton produces two styles of "Sac Chien," or dog carriers, for those who do not *parler francais*. . . . One style, sold only by department and specialty stores, is a small bag designed to hold a toy dog, exposing its head. This bag is shaped much like a woman's handbag and is a good choice for a small dog who accompanies a person during the day. The other design is far more versatile. It is accepted on airplanes and other means of conveyance, and is a smart replacement for the fiberglass containers supplied by the airlines. This bag comes in three sizes (13¾″ x 8″ x 10½″, 15¼″ x 8¼″ x 11¾″, and 17¾″ x 8¾″ x 13″), and is acceptable for travel within the coach of an airplane, but not for travel in the baggage compartment. Larger dogs can be accommodated with custom-made carriers, and a Louis Vuitton store can advise you on price and delivery of these specially made items.

by 6 foot lap pool. Athletic animals use the pool to refine their strokes. The dog paddle is *very* popular here. A swim can be followed by a soothing Jacuzzi bath. This relaxing treat is veterinarian-approved to be therapeutically beneficial after surgery, for hip dysplasia, for muscle fatigue after exercise, and for promoting healing of skin conditions.

The bath may be followed by a warm, dry sauna. The air flow is like a gentle warm breeze, and it's a quiet and calming way to complete your visit. Paunchy pets can pay for individual visits to the spa, or they may choose to become a full-time member of the center. In addition to visits, membership includes special discounts on supplies and gift items. Members also receive a specially designed jogging jacket with a Doggery Animal Center emblem applied, and the peo-

ple who referred the dog for membership receive a Doggery T-shirt. Dogs who are just beginning the Doggery regimen, or those who are not good in groups, may elect to work out with a trainer on a one-to-one basis. The spa can even come to your home to perform this special service.

Dogs on the run don't always take the time to stay physically fit. But the Doggery can bring its program home to you, through custom-made video tapes of your own exercise routine, filmed on location at the spa. These tapes can be played at home to provide an individualized video workout for those times when it's impossible to get to the gym. The Doggery Animal Center shapes itself to shape yourself . . . For further information, contact The Doggery Animal Center, 2462 Overland Avenue, Los Angeles, California 90064, (213) 553-4631.

(Continued on page 92)

She yearns for freedom and excitement.
Collar her.

RAVEL

Designer Luggage
(Continued from page 90)

Louis Vuitton luggage is available at the firm's own stores in the United States and abroad, and in select department and specialty stores. You may contact the firm's store in New York for the location of a store nearest you. Contact Louis Vuitton, 51 East 57th Street, New York, New York 10022, (212) 371-6111.

Mädler is another internationally recognized name for leather luggage. Its dog carrier is made of leather trimmed with a contrasting color for a sporty effect. The bag is available in a selection of colors and in two sizes, and it may be specially ordered if it is not currently in stock. To locate the store nearest you, contact Mädler, 450 Park Avenue, New York, New York 10022, (212) 688-5045.

Car rides are made more pleasant when you can look out the windows to watch the scenery. This simple-sounding feat was once accomplished through acrobatics for many small dogs perched upon laps, armrests, and rear windows, until the introduction of a car

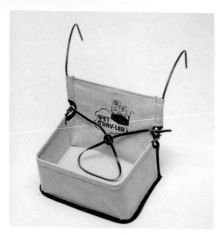

seat for small dogs. The Pet Trav-ler is a removable car seat with a safety harness to keep you in place during bumps or sudden stops. A foam seat lets you ride in comfort, and the 9″ x 12″ seating area holds a dog up to fifteen pounds. This simple device keeps any car pet from landing on the carpet. The Pet Trav-ler is available in pet shops and from the Sears catalog. If you require assistance in locating the seat, contact Foxy Fashions and Pet Accessories, 21311 Deering Court, Canoga Park, California 91304, (818) 716-7662.

Larger dogs, or any dog looking to ride in the car in safety, should remember to buckle-up. It's the law (for people) in many places. The Tag-A-Long pet seat belt lets you fulfill your civic duty to remain safe in your people's car. One end of the belt folds over the car's seat belt strap, and the one-piece harness goes across your chest. The seat belts are custom made to fit your measurements. To order yours, contact Tag-A-Long Traveler, Crossroads North, RFD 1, Box 111, Brewster, Michigan 56119.

Yacht-bound seadogs require special equipment to ensure a safe voyage on water. A dog life preserver will keep you afloat in the ocean, lake, or swimming pool. After all, some dogs, particularly the short-legged breeds like Scotties, are not skilled swimmers, and a life preserver is a good precaution to take when visiting aquatic areas. The life preserver illustrated comes in six sizes, keyed to chest measurements from 10″ to 34″. Adjustable buckles ensure a snug fit. The life jacket is available by mail order from the Pedigrees catalog, 15 Turner Drive, Spencerport, New York 14559, (716) 352-1232.

L'AIR DU CHIEN

horoscope

THE DOG DAYS' ASTROLOGICAL WEATHER

More than 2,000 years ago, the great heat of summer led to a superstition among the ancient Romans. They believed that the excessive heat, together with the increased disease and death associated with it, was somehow connected with the rising and setting of the star Canicula—the Little Dog. Accordingly, they conferred the name of "Dog Days" to the blazing months of July and August. This unfair and baseless calumny upon the good name of dogs has long since been disproved. Scientists observe that Canicula rises later and later each year; in millions of years, they predict, the star will actually herald the frost and snow of winter! Yet "the Dog Days" remains a popular phrase among insensitive people and will probably continue so for eons to come.

CAPRICORN December 22-January 20 Canine Capricorns are level-headed and practical. Old-fashioned values of hard work and honesty conceal a flirtatious side of animal magnetism and earthy sensuality. Your search for high standards extends to your choice of mate—you expect loyalty and won't settle for less.

AQUARIUS January 21-February 19 Aquarian animals are unconventional and ahead of the pack. You are brilliant, an innovative thinker who is always seeking a new challenge. (Your original ideas and imaginative solutions to problems are admired by all.) Self-motivated and charismatic, you seek to be unleashed to achieve your own success.

PISCES February 20-March 20 Pisces pups are cuddly and old fashioned. Always the idealistic dreamer, you look for protection, a dominant dog to rescue you from all life's little hassles. Because you have little or no wordly ambition, care nothing for rank or power, seldom succeed in making money, and rarely hold on to it when you do, you should think of spending your life as a poet, novelist, musician, artist, or dancer.

ARIES March 21-April 20 Fun-loving Aries animals are impetuous nonconformists. You are highly motivated, ambitious, and an efficent achiever, but your impulsive behavior can undermine your bright and perceptive

nature. Your loyalty is valued by all who know you, as is your lively spirit.

TAURUS April 21-May 21 Warm-hearted Taurans can be steadfast and practical puppies. Orderly and calm, you like to simplify things to reach solutions. Friends look to you for comfort and advice since you are the bark of reason in a constantly changing and often confusing world.

GEMINI May 22-June 21 Gemini dogs can be dual-natured. Changeable and capricious, the Gemini is self-motivated and individualistic. Charming and flirtatious, you don't always appear sensible to others, but you can succeed if you put your mind and paws to work.

CANCER June 22-July 23 Cancerian canines may appear snappish and emotionally on guard, but inwardly they are tender and caring. Your preference for home and family makes you the perfect litter mate and doghouse mother. When a Cancerian, like his crabby zodiacal sign, has seized an object (be it bone, ball, or Frisbee), he would rather lose a paw than let it go. This makes you a formidable tug-of-war opponent, as your humans undoubtedly know.

LEO July 24-August 23 Roar, puppy, roar! Leo dogs are born to lead, so you may as well let the world know it. Flashy and playful, you have enough razzle-dazzle glamour to get your own way. You know what you're doing,

and won't settle for less than your share of the goodies.

VIRGO August 24-September 23 Serious Virgo pups are idealistic, often setting high standards for themselves and others. You can be sexy and passionate with your mate, but others will see you as well organized and methodical, always in control and determined to reach your goal. Dull, maybe; but "Semper Fidelis Fido" is surely your motto.

LIBRA September 24-October 23 Charming, lively Libra has a ready laugh. You seem flirtatious and are easily bored and often unfocused. Often a lazy dog, you find the chase is better than the catch.

SCORPIO October 24-November 22 Sexy and magnetic, Scorpio begs for attention. You exude an air of mystery and have power over others. Whatever you want, you'll get—even if it means you have to growl and claw to get there.

SAGITTARIUS November 23-December 21 Sagittarius animals are bubbly and flamboyant. You are always involved in a new scheme and often achieve your goal—but in a zany, unconventional way. A flaky Fido, you bypass conventional methods to achieve success. There is, in fact, a curiously childlike transparency about you—probably because of the absence of complex emotions such as jealousy or vindictiveness—which makes you very easy to understand.

PUPIUM.
Pour celles qui s'aboyent à Yves Saint Bernard.

Parfums
YvesSaintBernard

DOGUE ®

Conceived and Written by
ILENE HOCHBERG

Designed by
FRANK MAHOOD

LAWRENCE GROW
Publisher, The Main Street Press

MARTIN GREIF
Editorial Director

Editors MARIANN ARNITZ, VICKI BROOKS **Art Director** FRANK MAHOOD
Art Associate JOHN D. FOX **Sales Manager** DONALD ROLFE **Promotion** BETSY NOLAN, MICHAEL POWERS **Corporate Marketing Director** IRWIN HOCHBERG

Photographers HANK LONDONER, PETER SERRA, JAMES PIPKIN, MARC RABOY
Models MORGAN, NUBIAN, ANNABEL, MORTIMER, BUBBLES, BUCHANAN, SPOT/SPIKE, ASTA, PIPER, SALLY, PUMPKIN, APRIL, KELLY, SHADOW, KIMBERLY, MILLIE, MUFFIN, GOLDIE

Fashion ILENE ROSENTHAL, JOANNE CAPALBO, NINA NAZIONALE
Beauty RICHARD HILLER, MEURET DIBRA, KAREN THOMPSON, JENNY McDONAGH, BRUCE LEE RESNICK, WAYNE FERGUSON, HALEY BIRK, NANCY JONES

Health BASHKIM DIBRA, WARREN and FAY ECKSTEIN, DEBBY SCHWARTZ, KITTY BROWN, JOANNE WILSON, LORETTA and RONALD GEE, STEVE GILMORE, CLAUDIA WOOLDRIDGE, BRIAN KILCOMMONS, PETER BORCHELT, LYNDA HUFFMAN

Living VINCENT RIENTI, SHIRLEY EPPS, CANNON GARBER, ANTHONY ELY-JOHNSTON, WILLIAM NICHOL, NANCY PLACE, LORI ENGLAND, PAT ZAJAC, TIM CURLIN, TOM ROSENBAUER, LUCIA VAN DER POST, GLYNN JENNON, MARY TERRY

Food LINDA COFFEY, GLORIA LISSNER, DREW McLANDRICH, SHAWN BADER, KAREN JARCZYNSKI, BEN RICHTER

Art KATHIE COMERFORD, J. GARVIN MECKING, JANE MILLETT, JULIE EVANS, FRIEDRICH GROSS, DUANE HANSON, WILLIAM WEGMAN, DONALD ROLLER WILSON, HOLLY SOLOMON, SAM PRATT, JIM and ANN MONTEITH, DIANA WASSERMAN

Features KITTY BROWN, MALCOLM KRIGER, GEORGE WARD, ROSALIND KRAUS, MARLENE LAMBERT, JUNE DUTTON, HEATHER HAMILTON, EDWIN SAYRES, Jr., ELINOR RUSKIN, NANCY HUANG, JAMES LILLEMOE

Travel CHRISTOPHER GRIEVSON, ANNABEL STEIN, AMANDA WINSTON, RITA STRATTA, BARBARA MEYERS, JACK ROSENSWEIG, BEVERLY HARKEY, JAMES KRACK, DONALD MENSH, ILSE PLOCKI, LILLIAN PAGAN, ANNE HOLLANDER, MARIE POIRIER, FRANCOIS DERAISME, SOPHY ROBINSON, JACKIE SPERANDIO, SUSAN GRADIJIAN, JOHN HOLLYWOOD

Dogue's Best Friends IRWIN HOCHBERG, TRUDY ROSENTHAL, CORRIE OSCHMANN, HOLLY and BARRY SILVERMAN, VAL TYLER, DONNA BIHELLER, CAROL HOCHBERG, LINDY and SETH HOCHBERG, GAIL and STEVE HOCHBERG, PHILIP ZOWINE, SUSAN PHILLIPS, JOANNE CAPALBO, LINDA CAHAN, STEVE BROWN, JEANNE and IRVING MATHEWS, STEPHANIE and HERBERT FREED, CICI and GEORGE ZAHRINGER, JOE RIGGIO and MARCELLE MARCHAND, DALE and KATHY VINCENT, MICHELLE and FRED DONER, CHRIS and STAN CANTOR, HANK and SUSAN LONDONER, BETH and EDDIE CRIMI, LESLIE OSCHMANN, TED EISEMAN, BASHKIM DIBRA, VINCENT RIENTI, RITA STRATTA, MARC RABOY, JOSEPH CICCIO, THOMAS NATALINI, DONALD MASSAKER, RICHARD HILLER, ROBERT EBERT, MONICA INCISA, MARIE SCHETTINO, NORRIS WOLFF, Esq., SPARKY ARNITZ, VINCENT CIANCIO, CHRISTOPHER GRIEVSON, ANNABEL STEIN, PATRICK JANSON-SMITH, DAVID KURFISS, ROBERT PEREZ, AMID BEN YEHUDA, KEN SEGAL, LEONORE FLEISCHER, LARRY ASHMEAD, MARGARET WIMBERGER, RAY PATIENT, TINA SNELL, ILSE HOCHBERG, ILENE ROSENTHAL, BERNARD ROSENTHAL, MALVINA and JOSEPH FARKAS

Published by Corgi Books, a division of Transworld Publishers Ltd., 61-63 Uxbridge Road, Ealing, London W5 5SA, in Australia by Transworld Publishers (Aust) Pty. Ltd., 15-23 Helles Avenue, Moorebank, NSW 2170, and in New Zealand by Transworld Publishers (N.Z.) Ltd., Cnr. Moselle and Waipareira Avenues, Henderson, Auckland.

First published in the United States by The Main Street Press.